HOTEL DESIGN

OTTO RIEWOLDT

Co-ordinating researcher
JENNIFER HUDSON

 LAURENCE KING

ACKNOWLEDGMENTS

The author, the co-ordinating researcher and the publishers would like to thank
Price Watkins for their elegant design of the book; Philip Cooper for his kind
and patient co-operation in editing this book; Yasuyuki Hirai for his dedicated
research for Japanese projects; all the architects and designers whose work
has been reproduced; and the various hotels and corporations that supplied
additional information on the projects featured.

Published 1998 by Laurence King Publishing
an imprint of Calmann & King Ltd
71 Great Russell Street
London
WC1B 3BN

A catalogue record for this book is
available from the British Library.

ISBN 1 85669 127 6

Designed by Price Watkins
Picture research by Jennifer Hudson
Printed in Hong Kong

Frontispiece: view of the Westin Regina Los Cabos Hotel,
San Jose del Cabos, Mexico

contents

new business hotels continued

resort and theme hotels   `132`

new grand hotels

introduction
grand venues, great ventures

A S WE approach the millennium, the hotel, that classic type of bourgeois architecture, is enjoying a striking revival. Parallels with its first golden age at the end of the 19th century are no coincidence. Then, in the *fin-de-siècle* spirit, the hotel was defined in aesthetic and social terms as a representative public space; today once again it has become a setting for social rituals and a mirror for contemporary myths. The context is different, of course: it is more global and democratic. In a world culture of mass tourism and media-influenced tastes, the forms and manifestations of contemporary hotel design are determined by marketing strategies and target-group segmentation. This manifest pluralism of style has a sound economic basis. In the Belle Epoque a single stylistic norm prevailed; today this is no longer the case, because of the diverse expectations and constantly changing leisure requirements of an ever more subtly differentiated clientele.

Catwalk and showcase
The hotel landscape is changing with astonishing speed. Within a few years a series of successful experiments had started a wide-ranging trend. What was still just theory and anticipation in the first survey of contemporary hotel design (Albrecht Bangert and Otto Riewoldt, *New Hotel Design*, London, 1993) has now become the norm in both conceptual and commercial terms. The quantum leap in design quality is at once a response to new customer demands and a stimulus to it. The days of drab, characterless functionalism are behind us.

The avant-garde design movement of the mid-1980s has matured in a remarkably short time, and now its influence has even reached the mainstream international chains. Now it is again accepted as the norm that hotels should provide more than just comfortable, standardized accommodation: first and foremost they should be unique public spaces, places for living and observing. They have recovered their role as a catwalk and showcase, where the guests move about in a theatrical setting, at once actor and audience, as encapsulated by sociologist Siegfried Kracauer in 1928: 'Hotels are filled with such figures in living colour. It almost seems as if they only live by the grace of an imaginary director'.

Alongside this development goes the rediscovery of the hotel as an attractive focal point for social activities. Not only for festivities, conferences and meetings, but also for the passing trade of the urban world. Restaurants, shopping arcades, health and fitness centres have all become important sources of revenue and occupy an ever more prominent place within the functional mix. The new city hotels have taken the concept of total care—as provided by all-inclusive resorts and vacation clubs—and reinterpreted this in their own way, by deliberately opening up to new customer groups. In fashionable cities like New York and London, extravagant lobbies with adjoining bars and restaurants have taken over from the once-dominant, trendy discothèques and bistros as the fashionable places to meet.

What counts, and what pays, is atmosphere. A hotel's ambience is its chief attraction and its defining quality in an increasingly competitive marketplace. The key concepts for success are individualization and diversification. At one end of the scale are the 'boutique hotels', often extremely focused and directed at connoisseurs of contemporary style, featuring highly distinctive design, contemporary art, or a mix of the two. At the other extreme are the synthetic fantasy worlds for holiday and entertainment, which use illusionistic overkill to satisfy a mass public fed on a constant diet of electronic images. Each of the various genres has its appropriate setting, like different theatres designed for different kinds of performance, from the intimate chamber piece to grand opera, from the kitsch cabaret to the avant-garde production.

Ethics as travelmate
Of course, the price-performance ratio has to be right at both ends of the scale: this almost goes without saying nowadays. After the downsizing of companies and state subsidies comes the streamlining of consumer lifestyles. Our awareness of cost and quality is increasing; our guilt about the conspicuous waste of natural resources is growing slowly, too. Now the mark of the true snob is doing without, focusing on the essentials, surfing luxuriously between exclusive simplicity and expensive understatement. Experiences are more important than products. Brand fetishism and the pressure to accumulate material goods are things of the past: in their place is the concept of 'lessness', encompassing an odd bundle of moral, ecological and élitist attitudes. Within this culture the consumer has something of a split personality, one minute opting for asceticism, the next for excess, or best of all for both at once, in a carefully modulated alternation.

This shift in values is embodied in a new type of specialist hotel, which turns the stress-victims of contemporary civilisation into contented patients with a mix of alternative medicine and New Age mysticism. There are shades of Hans Castorp, the voluntary invalid in Thomas Mann's novel *The Magic Mountain* , although today's magic mountains are set on the beaches of Thailand or other exotic locations. The search for personal well-being is mirrored in the ecologically motivated concern for endangered natural habitats. The last wild corners of the globe are being opened up as nature reserves for tourists. However absurd it may seem, this careful occupation, combined with a sensitive, sustainable approach to wildlife and plantlife, often represents their only chance of survival. Game lodges and wilderness resorts create a financial basis for the long-term preservation of the natural heritage. The rise of organic and natural products has prepared us for the idea that tourism mixed with ecological awareness is necessarily somewhat more expensive.

Until recently the global hotel chains were not noted for respecting local cultural traditions. As some of the examples in this book show, this is beginning to change. Now it is no longer enough simply to add a few ethnic touches to the conventional air-conditioned ostentation. The seriousness of this change of approach is evidenced by alliances with local architects and the use of local craftworkers: authenticity has become a marketing tool. On top of this, since the early 1990s, political and economic revolutions have brought regional changes of emphasis. With German reunification and the need to rebuild the former communist German state, the centre of design innovation moved eastwards to Berlin and other old cities like Dresden and Potsdam. South Africa, freed from apartheid, is seeing a boom in hotel building with a number of outstanding projects. However, for all their aspirations and record-breaking buildings, the top hotels in the Asian countries of Thailand, Malaysia, Singapore, Indonesia, Korea and Taiwan, fail to transcend a showy mediocrity, with just a few exceptions. There are still no highlights at all in developing countries like China, Russia and the former communist states of Eastern Europe.

Welcome to the niche

During his many reading tours, novelist Thomas Wolfe is supposed to have uttered the following lament: 'I have a horror of those small hotels and pensions with their mummified old gentlemen and ladies and their ugly furniture'. Today he would have no cause for complaint as the 'boutique hotels'–so named by New York entrepreneur Ian Schrager, one of their inventors–with their distinctive interior design and their prominently displayed contemporary works of art, have proliferated in number, offering beautiful contemporary settings where the world's beautiful people can feel at home.

The trend for the niche has reached beyond the hard core of design enthusiasts, and attracted the interest of an international following that is young, or at least young-at-heart. In the fashion world, adopting a particular designer or brand is like a declaration of faith; similarly, staying in hotels that display a particular design approach or artistic position is a statement of personal style and class. In the past the bourgeoisie celebrated social divisions in the pseudo-feudal setting of the grand hotels; today, designer hotels, hotels with the stamp of authenticity, are the chosen habitats of an initiated international 'in crowd'.

The main prerequisite for belonging to this group is not money but taste. Most of these projects are conceived on a small scale, and many are in the three- or four-star brackets. The hotels have founded their own booking association, Design Hotels International, which has been marketing reasonably priced, one-off designer hotels across the globe for a number of years. The downpricing is methodical: trendsetters like

Ian Schrager are targeting vertical customer groups. Schrager is now looking to take the process of democratization a step further: this hotel operator whose successes include hotels designed by Andrée Putman and Philippe Starck is currently planning to establish low-price 'Gap'-like hotels, set in the lower segment of the market, which will have a similar popular appeal similar to the eponymous American fashion chain.

Looking back over the steady rise of designer hotels since the 1980s, the present situation, as the first chapter shows, reveals considerable quality across the board, but only a few truly outstanding achievements. The avant-garde has not become tired, but just rather more laid back. The rhetoric has become more professional, hard-core didacticism has made way for subtle, often elegant settings. Sobriety and renunciation are still the order of the day, but they are playful and ironic, sometimes even deliberately old-fashioned. Showy décors and nostalgic ornaments sneak in, with a wink of conspiracy; fleamarket junk and classic design are jumbled together.

The mixture of contemporary interiors and contemporary art has been a clear success. The 'Teufelhof' in Basel, included in the earlier volume, had a gallery hotel extension added in 1996, and new works were installed in all the rooms in the existing section. In Germany the Art'otel group has expanded with projects in Dresden, Potsdam and Berlin, each as before dedicated to a famous contemporary artist. As well as investors and hotel enthusiasts, collectors and local politicians are beginning to take an interest in the projects combining hotel facilities and gallery space. In the centre of Düsseldorf, for example, a property investor with a valuable collection of modernist works is planning to build his own art hotel, by the year 2000, and the city council has donated the narrow plot for it.

First it was film stars and top models who discovered a new source of income with theme restaurants like Planet Hollywood and the Fashion Café; now the rock and pop élite has hit upon hotels as attractive investments. Members of the Irish band U2 invested in the Clarence Hotel in Dublin, the management company of Simply Red is co-financier of the elegant Malmaison hotel group, pop entrepreneur Chris Blackwell (who made his fortune with the Island Records label) has now opened nearly a dozen of his small Outpost hotels in the Caribbean and Florida. Yet mythical affinity between the temporary residence of the hotel and the restless lifestyle of the artistic bohemian has been given a new twist by these financiers from the modern-day musical world: the 'clean' style of today's designer hotels has about as much to do with the druggy decadence of New York's Chelsea Hotel or the Paris Beat Hotel as the squeaky-clean MTV culture has with the existential abysses of a Brendan Behan or William S. Burroughs.

Style counts

Of the three classic hotel genres–tourist hotel, spa hotel and city hotel–it was the last of the three that suffered most from the decline into functional banalities over the decades. Now, since the design wave reached the mainstream of the international hotel business, the pendulum is swinging back the other way with a vengeance. Now it is precisely the new generation of business hotels, presented in the second chapter, which is using design as a branding and marketing tool. Architecture and interior design are becoming an image factor for business and conference hotels, as they did in the office world transformed by the electronic revolution.

Design is acquiring an ever more vital importance as a way of distinguishing and defining hotels in the context of global competition for business travellers and conference participants. Unique, high-quality architects' designs are becoming a way of adding commercial value. The roll-call of architects commissioned with these projects reads like a who's who of contemporary architecture, featuring both established stars and highly promising newcomers. Hotels, once a neglected architectural genre, are now again at the forefront of the sector. The interior designs are not always up to scratch, however: successes like the ITT Sheraton Hotel at the Charles de Gaulle airport in Paris are still exceptional. The best results are generally achieved when architect and interior designer are one and the same.

Despite stagnating occupancy rates, the number of hotel rooms on the market continues to increase. Within a highly competitive market environment, the international hotel groups consider diversification as the key to success. New hotel types are being created as second or third brands, each with their own corporate identity and specialized design. French group Accor has perfected this formula for success with its budget chains like Ibis, Mercure and Formule 1, combining minimum stylistic input with highly impressive economic efficiency. Other companies have followed with ambitious projects of a similar nature: Hilton in the USA, for example, with the pavilion architecture of the Garden Inns, Steigenberger in Europe with the fashionable, colourful and low-price Maxx and Esprit hotels.

Cheerfulness, affordability and fresh designs are combined to form positive, motivating settings for business travellers. However, when business is slow even these brave new business hotels cannot avoid the effect described by Hermann Hesse in 1925: 'How maliciously, how demonically this friendly furniture, these well-meant carpets and these cheery wallpapers look at us!'

Safe adventures

The surrogate worlds provided by large-scale resort complexes and extravagant entertainment hotels are packed with the promise of pleasure and happiness. There are legions of them, with or without casinos and games machines. French philosopher Alain Finkielkraut describes these artificial paradises as 'places of collective regression', where the scenery of the entertainment industry and the kitsch paraphernalia of all continents and cultures are mixed together in a bizarre pot-pourri of attractions. It all began with Disney's fantasy parks; now Las Vegas has become the undisputed mecca of these megalomaniac excesses, with Polynesian islands and Roman temples, pirate islands and Wild West towns, Venetian gondolas and Egyptian pyramids, spitting volcanoes and a replica Manhattan.

In the past you had to travel to find exotic worlds: these pleasure domes provide instant, synthetic dreamworlds. In Japan, under huge glass domes, thousands of bathers splash around on tropical beaches, surrounded by palm trees and exotic foliage. The combination of show, gambling and fantasy hotel is a mass-market, family-friendly recipe for success which works just as well in the South African savannah as in the Bahamas. Musicals and Hollywood rehashes are the common currency for impresarios and investors. New York's run-down 42nd Street is being restored into an entertainment paradise, financed by Disney, with theatres, malls and a fun hotel by the Arquitectonica architects' team. Even in the German province of Swabia, near Stuttgart, a funfair city is growing up around two musical theatres, with hotel towers, multiplex cinemas and a water park.

As the third chapter shows, the gaudy, over-the-top entertainment business is only one manifestation of these safe adventures, even though it is the predominant one. The counter-movement, the romantic search for bolt holes away from the beaten tracks, is growing in importance. These special hideaways for those in the know can be round the corner on Santa Monica beach, in the last patches of African wilderness, or in a Caribbean bay. Some professionals in the luxury hotel business have caught on to this trend: they are using local colour and local culture to give their resorts a distinctive character.

Following in the steps of the omnipotent Disney, which has used famous architects for its entertainment projects since the 1980s, other clients are also involving prominent designers in their projects. Strict modernist Franklin D. Israel recently designed the Hard Rock Hotel for Las Vegas, and the postmodern wedding-cake style of Michael Graves will soon be on view by the Red Sea in Egypt.

Desire for luxury

Globetrotter and bon-viveur Ernest Hemingway is supposed to have said 'When I dream of an afterlife in heaven it is always set in the Ritz'. This grand hotel in Paris was and remains the paradigm of which just a few historic landmarks survive. Today the genre is seeing a revival, with a diverse array of imitations. However, nostalgia-laden imitation palaces loaded with eclectic historical reproductions are no longer the only option for providing the international jet-set with suitably luxurious places to stay. The renaissance of this bourgeois architectural genre has in some cases spawned a thoroughly up-to-the-minute modernism, as in the Four Seasons in New York, designed by I.M. Pei, and a few of the more recent Park Hyatt projects.

The conservatism can do without clichéd ostentation and wall-to-wall gilding: instead it strives for cultural variety and a new high-class style vocabulary, often following in the Art Deco tradition. Elegance here is based on the art of selection and exclusivity. The grandeur of the grand hotels was never just a question of size, and today there are small-scale projects which consciously cultivate a classy, exclusive intimacy. In these projects we can see a return to the early meaning of the word 'hotel', when it designated an upper-class town house, a million miles from the functional and undistinguished places (inns or boarding houses) which accommodated ordinary travellers.

As the fortunes of the hotel sector have risen and fallen, the top class has remained relatively stable. Operators within this category have even been moving into the world's emerging markets: the new Grand Hyatt for the millennium is to be located in Shanghai, in the tallest building in the world. Five-star hotels are a solid investment even for groups like the troubled Kempinski chain, which has recently changed hands a number of times. This group has acquired the top addresses in the former East Germany with the historical Taschenbergpalais in Dresden, the venerable Fürstenhof in Leipzig and the legendary Adlon in Berlin.

Bed and netfast

A few years ago only a few very forward-looking hotel operators provided their guests with the computer and telecommunications equipment of the modern age, either in business centres or in the rooms themselves. Today it is the norm for modern hotel designs to incorporate all the latest information technology. Hotels in Japan and in the southern Asian cities of Singapore and Hong Kong were the first to provide high-quality electronic facilities, with multiple telephone lines, digital equipment and data services. Now even mid-class establishments in the USA and Europe have followed suit.

Televisions and other forms of electronic entertainment can be incorporated in any living environment, and computers and cables will function in any type of office—in the same way, digital communications technology can be integrated with the hotel atmosphere. Guests can surf the internet from the comfort of their bed, whether the bed in question has soft victoriana pillows or a hard futon mattress. Global operators in the hotel sector are addressing these progressive concepts with rooms that respond interactively to users' needs, calling them 'smart rooms' (ITT Sheraton) or 'Rooms that work!' (Marriott Group).

These new approaches reflect the belief that mobility, professionalism, working and hotels belong together and that the travelling executives of today must be provided with the electronic equipment they need. It remains to be seen how far this multimedia invasion of the hotel sphere will promote, transcend or erode the sensuality so eloquently described by author Anaïs Nin (and this may depend on the possibilities of cyberspace): 'The room was pleasant, friendly, movingly imperfect. But it had a mysterious radiance, filled with erotic brilliance and past guests. Words had been exchanged here, gestures had been made. Love was made with wit and imagination, wine was drunk, dreams were dreamed, and bodies and delicate suppers exuded their warmth'.

Home from home

Hotel experts agree that in the short term the majority of additional investments will be devoted to improvements in room quality. Here too the strategy of differentiation is apparent. Rooms will not just be defined according to their size and level

of comfort, they will also be targeted at specific customer groups. Offering a broad range of services has clear competitive benefits, and these days it is more than just a question of segmenting smokers and non-smokers: now there are irritant-free rooms for allergy-sufferers, rooms with fitness equipment for health fanatics, rooms with play areas for families with children. There are also more rooms and facilities suitable for people with disabilities. Lobbies and other areas which do not directly generate revenue are being cut back to make way for restaurants, shops, health clubs and other profitable services.

The hotel room is becoming a temporary home, a *pied-à-terre*, a place not just for staying the night but for working and doing business. Apartment hotels like the Marriott Group's Residence Inn, the French Citadines and the German Madison hotels are the forerunners of a growing trend. Here the standard furnishings are adaptable, with convertible elements that enable guests to turn a sleeping space into a work room in a matter of seconds. Room-in-room concepts, mobile partitions and built-in kitchens are all part of the design, as are computer and telecommunications facilities. Here, the hotel room is a multifunctional area for working, relaxing, leisure—a place for business, recreation and fun. Buildings combining hotels and part-time offices are becoming increasingly common.

The conditions of the information age are changing the hotel landscape as we approach the end of the millennium, and at the same time they are confirming the essential purpose of hotels for travellers. Worldwide communications networks and the virtualization of work and leisure are increasing mobility and fragmenting living conditions. Everyday life is dominated by the temporary, by changing preoccupations, settings, jobs and attractions. For all their innovation, in terms of atmosphere the new functional, architectural and design solutions are perpetuating what Vicki Baum appropriately defined as a place of destiny in her classic novel *People in Hotels* in 1929: 'That which is experienced in a great hotel does not comprise well-rounded, full, completed destinies, but rather fragments, shreds, pieces. Behind its doors are people, ordinary or remarkable, people on the way up, people in decline; bliss and catastrophe live cheek by jowl. The revolving door turns, and what is experienced between arrival and departure is not a whole. Perhaps there are no whole destinies in the world, only approximations; beginnings that lead nowhere, endings preceded by nothing. And what happens behind the doors of life is not rigid like the columns of a work of architecture, or predetermined like the structures of a symphony, or predictable like the course of the stars. It is human, fleeting, and more difficult to grasp than the shadows of clouds drifting over a meadow'.

The transitory is inscribed in the hotel architecture of today as much as it ever was, but with all its unpredictability contemporary hotel design certainly does not promise any new aesthetic completeness. The plurality and quality are encouraging signs for the future: the outlook is more promising than ever.

designer and art hotels

Since the pioneering achievements of the 1980s the avant-garde
has lost none of its steam, it has just become rather more
laid back. And with good reason: its aesthetic statements can
now count on support reaching beyond the hard core of design
enthusiasts, attracting the growing interest of an international
clientele that is increasingly young, or at least young at heart.
What was at first a purely city-based phenomenon has now
become a much more broad-based and diversified movement
reaching into the heart of the provinces. Customers are drawn to
these temples of contemporary style in the search for a direct
confrontation with authentic design creations, whether these be
the interiors of designer hotels, or the contemporary art works
that form the centrepiece of art hotels. In terms of size, most of
these projects are conceived on a relatively small scale,
appropriate to the élite group of customers they are targeting.
Once again Philippe Starck, the star designer also famous for
his product designs, is the exception that proves the rule here:
his recent hotels in the United States break the mould
in terms of size and design quality, setting standards that his
eager band of imitators cannot hope to equal.

Mondrian

Los Angeles, USA, 1996

Interior Designer: Philippe Starck

THE Mondrian on West Hollywood's Sunset Boulevard already has quite a past behind it: built as an apartment block in 1959, converted to a hotel in 1984, and then radically overhauled by Philippe Starck a dozen years later. In the mid-1980s it was briefly regarded as the height of fashion, with its coloured façade modelled on the abstract geometrical patterns of the Dutch De Stijl painter Piet Mondrian. But the design aged rapidly, and it fell to hotel duo Ian Schrager and Philippe Starck to transform this faded homage to a modernist classic into a striking manifestation of contemporary style. Schrager, a canny and adventurous hotel entrepreneur from New York, picked up in Los Angeles where he had left off in New York and Miami, moving up a gear at the same time. Starck, the star designer from Paris, was in his element and created

Below: Oversized and free standing red steel 'doors' offer the first glimpse of Starck's paradoxical playful use of scale

another masterpiece which none of his growing band of imitators can hope to emulate.

Starck whitewashed over the yellow, red and blue squares on the front façade and added two huge red steel doors with ornamental handles in front of the entrance, creating behind it a wonderland worthy of Alice or Gulliver. The design concept is a joyful improvisation, with witty thematic variations on the myths, illusions and fictions of this city of dreams. Hollywood is not directly quoted, though: Starck's designs focus on the ambiguity, the deceptive seductiveness and the surreality of this world of surrogates and fantasies. Alienation effects are used to alter perception; sudden changes of scale and magical light effects form the unsettling vocabulary of the design. There is an illuminated marble table, no less than twenty metres long; guests eat on the pool deck in an alley of gigantic earthenware flowerpots, from which climbing plants grow up to form a flowering canopy over their heads. Light projections imitate carpets, shadowy indirect beams of light make walls and fittings appear to float in mid air. Starck created this subtle symphony of light with the help of some famous assistants: mysterious installations by no less than James Turrell shimmer in the lobby, video images by chic video clip director Jean-Baptiste Mondino flicker in the lifts.

Yet the Mondrian also displays a loving indulgence in the simple things of life: plain, broad wooden floorboards, huge beds, a roof terrace with swimming pool and restaurant furnished like a friendly open-air drawing room. The rooms – of which there are 245, including suites and apartments – cultivate a cheerful simplicity, the furnishings are kept to the bare minimum. It was fortunate that the original kitchens in the rooms had survived the passing of time: now they are an integral component of the concept of chic hotel as temporary home.

Schrager paid $ 17 million to acquire this Californian property, and invested at least as much again in the conversion. For this lavish outlay the Mondrian now has everything an avant-garde hotel needs to spoil its illustrious guests. Half a dozen different types of cuisine, a 24-hour health club and a mind-body studio run by the New-Age-inspired wife of film producer Peter Guber. Moderate prices indicate that this magical, understated luxury is not just intended for the happy few, and Schrager describes his target public in similarly broad terms: 'In this new era of uncomplicated sophistication, Mondrian will attract a vertical market based more on attitude, values and style than on financial considerations'.

Preceding pages: (on the left) Door
leading to the elevator area.
The wooden floor matches the lift
frames which are enhanced by
soft-lit curtains. The lobby diner
space (on the right) is dominated
by a 20-metre-long marble table

Below: The bedrooms are havens
of simple comfort with
spare, free standing furniture.

The manipulation of scale is duplicated by two parallel rows of 2-metre-high garden pots which separate the restaurant and the pool area and form a canopied area for al fresco dining.

The neutral materiality of the public areas is flooded with magic lighting effects creating a thrilling ethereal world. The table and bench set by Droog Design and Mr Chia's moulded resin sofa form part of an international collection of over 200 pieces of designer furniture contained within the hotel.

The roof-top pool is bordered by huge plate-glass windows offering bathers a glimpse of downtown Los Angeles. The chemical-free pool with classical music piped from underwater speakers is flush with the surrounding deck.

Delano

Miami Beach, USA, 1995

Architecture: PMG Architects

Interior Design: Philippe Starck

Starck's 'tropical Oasis far from the rat-race of everyday life' is a mixture of theatricality and simple elegance. Below: Lobby seating arrangement. Right: The pool area called the Water Salon.

NEW YORK entrepreneur Ian Schrager chose one of the larger specimens among Miami Beach's countless Art Deco and 1950s hotels to continue the success story he had begun so impressively in the mid-1980s with New York design icons The Morgan, The Royalton and The Paramount. As with the last two projects, he commissioned the cult French designer Philippe Starck to produce the entire interior decoration of the 16-storey building, which dates from 1947.

According to Schrager, each decade has its own characteristic venue: in the 1970s it was discothèques, in the 1980s it was restaurants, and now in the 1990s it is the turn of hotels. His theory is confirmed by his worldwide following: the inventor of designer hotels now has a growing and eager band of disciples. However, the ideal partnership with Starck puts Schrager several lengths ahead of the rest of the field. The Delano demonstrates this both in its grand gestures and in its small details.

Here Starck celebrates his version of 'simple chic' in a relaxed and entirely inimitable fashion. No self-references, no pretentious inflation of his New York icons, just the perfect, airy beach hotel. All the loud, overcharged hustle and bustle of the infamous South Beach is simply refused admission: 'In some ways the reality of Miami is terrible, poisoned by the scourges of venality, exhibitionism, reckless ambition. Therefore I tried to make the Delano into a kind of opposite, similar to the image of a tropical oasis, far from the rat-race of everyday life. Through spaces and objects with a soul, discreet but friendly presences, I have sought to make guests feel comfortable, stimulating to make them more happy, or at least to be actors and not just spectators, as advertising and the media would have it' (Starck).

Theatrical imagery is all around as soon as you enter the Delano. The lobby areas are divided by light gauze curtains, the furniture and fittings are arranged like haphazardly assembled props and scenery from some long-forgotten play. The canopy-covered terrace forms a theatrical interlude which is followed by a change of scenery in the open-air stage of the pool area, called the Water Salon. However, the gentle, vivacious theatricality of the public areas does not continue in the guest rooms, where brilliant, pure brightness predominates: the walls, floors, ceilings and furniture are all white. Yet there is no hint of clinical sterility here: the old-fashioned whimsicality of the furnishings is more reminiscent of Maxim Gorki's *Summer Folk* than a hospital. The Delano is full of happy surprises: not only 238 rooms, lofts, suites, apartments and bungalows, but also an orchid garden. Not only restaurants and bars inside and out but also the macrobiotic Blue Door owned by the pop goddess Madonna. Not only the David Barton Gym but also, on the roof, a beauty centre called Agua offering baths, massage and cosmetic therapies. The Women's Bath House is closed to men: it is a 'paradis des dames' in the sky.

The lobby leads the guests through
a succession of stage sets.
This part features the Eat-in kitchen.

In contrast to the public areas the guest rooms are custom-painted white or pearly grey. Starck has studiously 'under-designed' the furniture, lamps and bathroom fittings which nonetheless offer high style, comfort and intimacy.

Hotel New York

Rotterdam, Netherlands, 1993

Interior Design: Dorine de Vos

ROTTERDAM'S Wilhelminakade is a piece of transatlantic shipping history. It was from this pier, from 1873 onwards, that European emigrants embarked on their steamship journey to the New World. This was where the Holland-Amerika Lijn (HAL) had its headquarters, in a brick building constructed shortly after the turn of the century. The shipping line finally closed down in 1978: the docks of the Kop van Zuid (framed by two branches of the Maas River) could not compete with modern container shipping and closed shortly after. HAL moved to Seattle, and its building went up for sale, desolate and abandoned in the midst of the disused quayside, until Rotterdam's city authorities decided to turn this wasteland into an urban renovation area.

A series of major projects was devised, featuring a number of highly-reputed architects. However, the first marker on the road to renewal came not from these famous names, but from ten enterprising Rotterdamers, who formed a collective to acquire the former HAL headquarters, converted it into the lively Hotel New York with a budget of 11 million Guilders, and who still take an active part in the management today. Dorine de Vos, Hans Loos and Daan van der Have were the trio responsible for the project. De Vos took the leading role in designing the interiors: 'We wanted to create the kind of hotel where we ourselves would like to stay, where you really feel the sensation of travelling. An essential starting point in creating this sensation was the location, the building, its history. The spaciousness, the atmosphere and view of the river would determine the feeling of luxury. Hotel New York does not try to nostalgically picture the atmosphere of the hotels of former times, but to realise, in its own way, the hospitality and elegance of travelling in days gone by'.

De Vos's affection for the building's heritage was such that the old Art Nouveau carpets from the directors' offices were carefully restored and now adorn the conference rooms and guest rooms. The interiors have been pieced together with an instinctive sureness of taste. Antiques from the flea market are mixed with cheap-and-cheerful Ikea furnishings and the odd designer creation. Sparkling chandeliers can be seen alongside modern classics. The hotel operations are relatively modest, with 72 rooms on three floors, a tower suite and a penthouse suite. The heart of the building is the ample, lively café-restaurant, which has 400 seats in all, including an oyster bar, a tea room and a winter garden. The interior design hovers between romanticism and pragmatism in a thoroughly attractive mix, typical of contemporary Dutch style. In its own relaxed way it provides everything a hotel needs to make its guests feel at home, faithfully following Dorine de Vos's motto: 'Mixed style, only the necessary and a very good bed!'

Above: The Hotel New York is accommodated in the former headquarters of the Holland-Amerika Lijn shipping company.

Right: Section

Opposite page: The guest rooms recall the luxury of the bygone age of travel. By using a mixture of flea-market finds, shop-bought furniture, a few designer pieces and restored *art nouveau* carpets Dorine de Vos has successfully reinvented the language of bric-a-brac chic.

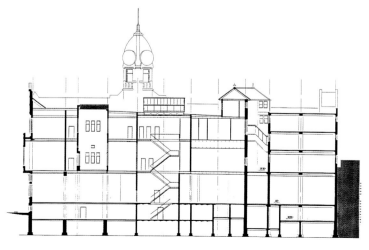

Above: The conference room located on the old Directors' floor is dominated by a wall of huge windows allowing panoramic views of the River Maas and the harbour surrounds.

Below: Colourful glazed tiles and simple white fittings make up the basic charm of the bathrooms.

The maritime and leisure theme is found throughout the hotel. Ship lights and sunsails decorate the main corridor

The Brunswick Hotel

Glasgow, Great Britain, 1995

Architecture: Elder & Cannon Architects

Interior Design: Graven Images

GLASGOW'S new Brunswick Hotel is contained within a narrow gap between buildings in the old commercial district on the eastern edge of the city. Despite a carefully shaped roof extension, the design by local architects Elder & Cannon is remarkably indecisive in its effect, hovering somewhere between reverence to its historical surroundings and modernist resistance. There are pragmatic reasons for the compact functionality of this Scottish version of the designer hotel: 'Economic viability dictated a taller structure than the previous three-storey building which occupied the site. The resulting form extends through eight floors which are divided vertically into three distinct zones, expressed externally by changes of material and form' (Elder & Cannon).

A budget of £1.1 million does not leave much room for artistic licence, even in a small city hotel of 1,000 square metres. This is also true of the interior design,

created by the Graven Images team from Glasgow. The client, Primavera Leisure, bravely cites the fashionable Royalton and Paramount hotels in New York as its models: however, the fact that these aspirations remained beyond the reach of the architects was not merely attributable to budgetary constraints. The Scottish pretenders could not match the style and inventiveness of a Philippe Starck. Nonetheless, they have produced a creditable achievement within the bounds of what was possible.

The tripartite division of the hotel front signals the different functional zones: below, behind display windows, are the reception and restaurant; above this is the stone façade of the guest-room storeys (a total of 18 small rooms with shower or mini-bathroom); finally on the two top floors there is the relatively spacious, copper-clad penthouse suite. Apart from this ample maisonette, the interior designers' brief was to make optimum use of the available space. In the ground floor and the basement they were able to disguise the lack of space through the clever use of furniture and changes in ceiling height. In the euphemistically-named Metro Suites – the bedrooms – conditions are positively claustrophobic. There was no room for anything but the bed, a fitted wardrobe and tiny wall cupboards. To the designers' credit, their carefully thought-out furnishing plan ensures that these guest rooms nonetheless have a friendly atmosphere.

Maybe the designers were correct in their assessment of their target public: 'We always saw the project as a hybrid. It is aimed at a mix of people who, irrespective of wealth, share and understand a common ideology. They have probably travelled enough to appreciate simplicity' (Graven Images). The entrepreneurs of Primavera Leisure will hope that they are right about the motivation of their potential customers: the Brunswick is intended as the prototype for a chain of city hotels that is soon to be exported beyond the Scottish borders.

Left: The Brunswick was designed to fit into a narrow gap between existing period buildings. The façade is stylistically divided into three parts reflecting the different functions of the internal spaces. The copper-clad roof extension contains the penthouse suite.

Opposite: The bar/restaurant and private dining area are incorporated on the ground floor behind display windows. An illusion of height is created by the use of different ceiling levels, concealed lighting and artful modelling.

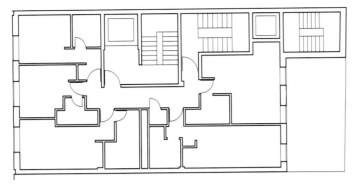

Normal guest room floor plan

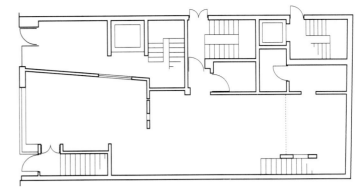

Ground floor plan

The limited site severely restricted the size of
the guest rooms. Clever design of storage
space and furnishings have nonetheless created
a comfortable atmosphere.

Left : The tiny reception area is in muted tones. The use of colour is an important tool in the differentiation of internal spaces within the Brunswick.

Below: The split-level and airy penthouse suite contrasts with the compact guest rooms. The use of light wooden floor, white walls and selected pieces of contemporary furniture complements the simplicity of the design concept

Das Triest

Vienna, Austria, 1995

Architecture/Interior Design: CD Partnership, Sir Terence Conran, James Soane

....

FOR a long time Trieste was the only sea port in the entire Austrian empire, and the road between Vienna and this foothold on the Adriatic was a very busy one. In Vienna, the coachmen and their horses lodged in quarters and stables outside the city wall on the Wiedner Hauptstraße. When the coaches were replaced by steam engines and then by cars, the 300-year-old site became a convent; later it was converted into the hotel Stadt Triest. It was Alexander Maculan, an Austrian building magnate who has since gone bust, who decided to give the run-down property a new and

Right: Axonometric of the public areas.

Opposite page, top: The open inner-courtyard is flanked by two old stable blocks housing the restaurant to the right and conference facilities to the left.

Opposite page, bottom: The vestibule with rounded Porter's desk, and green and white marble floor. Restrained elegance offers a well needed antidote to the Baroque extravaganzas of the five-star hotels typical of Vienna

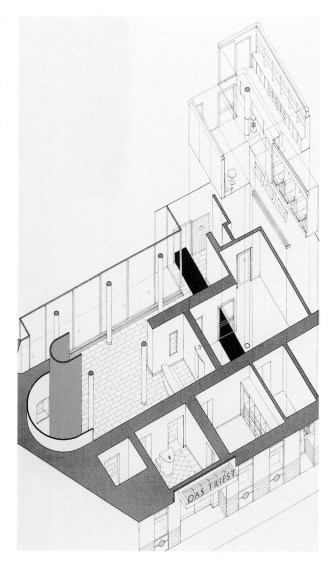

elegant lease of life. After a number of designs had been proposed, he decided to approach Sir Terence Conran, the design entrepreneur who had achieved such success with his London restaurants, to see if he would like to try his hand at hotel design.

Conran's CD Partnership took on the project and defined their aim as follows: 'A hotel is a place where both fantasy and reality reside side by side. A place where design and detail are integral to the whole experience. The thematic approach was to develop an attitude towards luxury and comfort that was not overt, opulent or vulgar. In some ways it was a reaction to the Viennese tradition of Baroque that has degenerated today into faded kitsch' (project architect James Soane).

The six-storey forebuilding, with its restrained modern style of design, certainly displays no great respect for the imperial heritage. Only beyond the entrance and the lobby do guests encounter any traces of the past. The open, inner courtyard is flanked by two old stable wings, which now house the restaurant and conference rooms. The only historical feature to remain untouched was the brick vaulting of the basement, which was made into a wine cellar.

The hotel, succinctly named Das Triest, has a total of 73 rooms and suites. Except for a few chairs, the entire interior was designed by Conran's team. Photographs on the walls show what the old Vienna-Trieste coach route looks like today. The spartan chic and the colour scheme of yellow, blue and white were designed to offer an alternative to the conventional five-star opulence that is typical of the area. The hotel's target clientele is the international artistic jet set – art directors, media professionals, photographers, models and the like – who are increasingly using Vienna as a starting point for expeditions into the former communist states of Eastern Europe. This successful venture into hotel design had positive consequences for the CD Partnership, who have since worked on a number of other similar projects.

Right: The brick, barrel-vaulted wine bar was once the storage cellar and is the only part of the original coach house structure kept intact.

Below: The marble stairwell is flooded with bright light, which enhances the use of white stone and bleached woodwork. It winds around a green wall punched with portholes lined in gold leaf.

Opposite page: An area off the lobby uses cherry wood and opaque glass screens to add an element of privacy for apéritifs before dining in the adjacent restaurant.

The Hempel

London, Great Britain, 1996

Architecture/Interior Design: Anouska Hempel and Anouska Hempel Designs

AFTER the biedermeier-style excesses of Blakes Hotel, opened by Anouska Hempel in 1996, the last thing you would have expected from this interior designer and couturière was an austere, oriental-style contemporary retreat in the Zen ascetic mode. This radical change of approach reflects not so much the project's Japanese financial backing as a general change of mood, which some see as a fund-amental shift in values and others simply as a fashion for 'lessness'. And Lady Weinberg, to use Anouska Hempel's full title, is once again at the head of the field, moving from the over-the-top largesse of the 1980s to the extravagant and no less expensive renunciation rituals of the 1990s. The project is a striking success. Behind the perfectly preserved stucco façades of five Georgian terraced houses in Bayswater, a formalized, geometrical and monochrome temple world opens up.

The hotel, simply named The Hempel, conveys its spiritual message with a stunning, positively cathartic consistency. The high priestess herself recounts her Damascus experience in Egypt: 'One day I came out of a pyramid and knew exactly what I was going to do. That first vision did not change. It is the result of a desire for radical change. I want to evoke the serenity of the East. I don't want any art on the walls, I want it completely blank, so the quality of the stonework and plasterwork can speak for itself. I'm trying to get rid of the word "minimalism", which makes people think it's not comfortable. We just call it modernism, pared-down architecture or hempelism!'.

Without completely gutting the five existing buildings this purist effect could not have been created. The striking effect of the atrium foyer, which opens up with unexpected spaciousness behind the bourgeois façades, produces extreme responses in visitors. Either they are captivated, indeed over-whelmed, by the intense beauty of the celebrated emptiness – or they find it cold and hard and want to get out as quickly as possible. However, for the initiated, for the devotees of expensive austerity, The Hempel is a revelation.

White is the dominant colour, varied only with black lines, areas and fittings, and with the natural shades of wood and hemp. The main materials used are light Portland stone, granite, Canadian Douglas pine and American oak. Within this strict overall style the 44 rooms and 6 apartment suites are individually designed, all of them perfect examples of 'Zen luxury' in practice. In the basement are the Italian-Thai gourmet restaurant 'I-Thai', and the 'Shadow Bar' which offers high-class snacks: these are reached by a narrow flight of stairs illuminated by subtle plays of light. With all the will in the world there was no way you could fit a proper sacred grove in a Bayswater terrace, so Hempel did the next best thing and bought up the whole square behind it, Craven Hill Gardens, now Hempel Garden Square. With its square pools of water bordered by square patches of gravel and square lawns, this is an oasis for meditation – disturbed only by the very mundane racket of traffic noise and parking cars.

Left: The Hempel Garden with small square pools surrounded by pure white gravel and symmetrically placed garden furniture

Opposite: The 'reduced architecture' of the spacious reception foyer with open fireplaces and the pureness of the Portland stone

The bedrooms demonstrate Anouska Hempel's Zen style with spartan elegance in black and white. The kimono is repeatedly used as a symbol of happiness and wealth.

The Shadow bar is
situated in the
basement. The diving
board at its centre hovers
above a sea of polished
zebrite slate

The bathroom carries on
the theme of eastern
tranquillity; its asceticism
is cathartic.

Art'otel

Dresden, Germany, 1995

Architecture: Rolf and Jan Rave

Interior Design: Dennis Santachiara

THE painter A. R. Penck left Dresden for the West after falling out of favour with the cultural police in the former GDR, and subsequently became one of the most famous German artists on the international scene. Now he has come home, in an unusual way: the building dedicated to him in his home town is not a gallery or a museum but a new hotel in the latest Italian style. Opened in 1995, it houses 694 paintings, graphic works and sculptures by Penck.

The Epicurean Penck is far less bothered than strict art connoisseurs might imagine to see his expressive line figures, reminiscent of cave-paintings, in such a resolutely contemporary setting. The hotel follows the concept devised by investor Dirk Gädeke for his small chain of Art'otels: guests are given a unique opportunity to get to know the work of a major artist during their stay. Gädeke rejects conventional hotel decoration (with its miscellaneous assemblies of artefacts) in favour of facilitating a direct encounter with key figures of the contemporary art scene. The project began in 1990 with the work of the Happening/performance artist Wolf Vostell at the Art'otel Sorat in Berlin; it has now grown to include hotels not only in Dresden but also in Potsdam and most recently in another one in Berlin. The hotels transform an élitist, upmarket pursuit into a democratic, unobtrusively personal encounter with art.

Milan designer Dennis Santachiara, who took part in Documenta 1987, was commissioned to design the interior of the Art'otel Dresden; he was aware of the ambivalence of his task: 'My intention in collaborating on this project was to apply to the dimension of design those aesthetic relationships which characterize my own objects: an expansion of perception with the purpose of surprising the visitor in a poetical manner, with the aid of little magic effects and with poetical performances. In the decisions taken for the designs of these rooms with the absolutely perceptible presence of art, I have accordingly sought out aesthetics not only in the design itself but also with respect to the questions of what the objects do and how they do it (as a way of bringing aesthetics to life)'. Art may take centre stage in this hotel but Santachiara did not see this as requiring a subservient, reverential attitude on his part. Not for him the whitewashed anonymity of conventional galleries: on the contrary he designed spaces that are colourful and attractive in themselves.

The functional context of the hotel presents an elegant and stimulating contrast to the elemental energy of Penck's pictures. The artist himself even responded directly to the building: the monumental murals in the foyer were produced not in the studio but on site. A short illuminated pathway leads from here to the neighbouring Kunsthalle Dresden, which is also used as a venue for business events. The artistic works have a prominent but not overpowering place in the 174 rooms and in the Factory Restaurant with its adjoining bar. The Art'otel is set within a triangular city-centre complex also designed by Rolf and Jan Rave.

Left: The rather plain architectural style of the building acts as a foil to the extravagant and colourful interiors.

Opposite: The main foyer with wall paintings by A. R. Penck and the flamboyant interior design style of Dennis Santachiara

Left: Guest room with wooden panelling and integrated lighting.

Below: Restaurant with fabric sails and customized furniture

Above: The Art'otel is connected to the 630-square-metre Kunsthalle by a series of stairs and walkways.

Left: The ground floor plan of the building shows the multi-functional uses of the hotel, the art gallery, various shops and restaurants as well as office spaces.

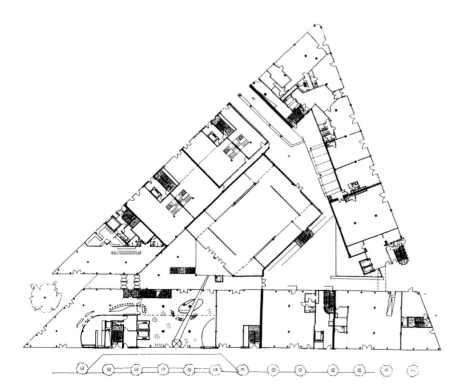

Art'otel

Potsdam, Germany, 1995

Architecture: Rolf and Jan Rave

Interior Design: Jasper Morrison/Axon, Beate Weller

THE old royal seat of Potsdam and the idyllic landscape around it, along the River Havel, are among the jewels of Prussia: here the state's rulers, while single-mindedly expanding their empire through politics and warfare, built castles and parks of extraordinary beauty. Even the everyday buildings they constructed reflected their elevated artistic ideals. An example of this functional architecture, with pretensions to grandeur, is the flour mill designed by Ludwig Persius, a follower of Schinkel, in 1843. This Romantic architect turned the functional building into a castle: the steam engine's tall chimney became a soaring defensive tower, while the granary was crowned with battlements. The mill was operational until the Red Army arrived in 1945; after this it was used successively as a bakery, slaughterhouse, chicken-coop and furniture store.

With the end of the communist régime and German reunification, the building saw an upturn in its fortunes. Dirk Gädeke, the Berlin property developer who had achieved success with his hotel projects combining contemporary art and ambitious interior design, discovered the royal mill building and saw in it a promising investment opportunity. The architects Rolf and Jan Rave revitalized this historical monument and added a new four-storey wing. The English minimalist Jasper Morrison was commissioned to design the interior, while the art works were provided by Katharina

Sieverding, professor at the art academy in Düsseldorf, and the German representative at the Venice Biennale of 1997. Interior designer Beate Weller, from the Frankfurt studio Axon, was responsible for co-ordinating the work of these different contributors.

The three-star hotel has 123 rooms and suites. The ground floor of the new building houses the foyer, the bar and the Aqua fish restaurant. The conference rooms are in the upper storey of the old granary, while the health club is lodged right at the top, under the gabled roof. The hotel has its own launch for guests who wish to explore the beauties of the landscape from the river. With the Art'otel in Potsdam Gädeke was pursuing his aim of combining different arts, which he first formulated in the early 1990s: 'The design concept is to be viewed as a homage to the artist. The combination of art with contemporary design and architecture makes every Art'otel a work of art in itself. Art'otel appeals to the intelligence and artistic interests of its guests as the key to a unique experience. The stay arouses emotions and stimulates reflection on artistic themes and perhaps even on social values'. In Potsdam, Morrison's reductionist asceticism and Sieverding's series of mirrored frames and photographs (specially created for the hotel) complement each other in their detachment from the Romantic heritage. Both artists present variants of a very European quest for a new artistic identity.

Right and opposite, below: Exterior and ground-floor plan showing the relationship between Rolf and Jan Rave's new hotel wing and the original flour mill designed by Ludwig Persius.

**Above: The foyer is housed in the
ground floor of the new building.**

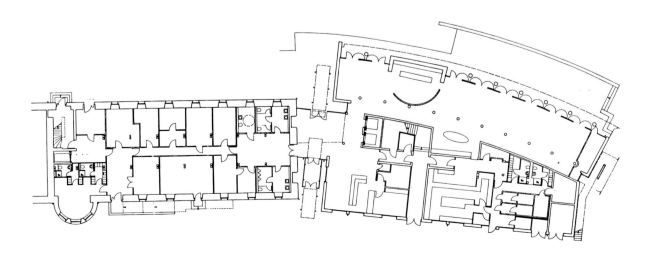

Above: This quite and discreet public area is typical of Jasper Morrison's restrained style of design.

Right: A typical guest floor ground plan.

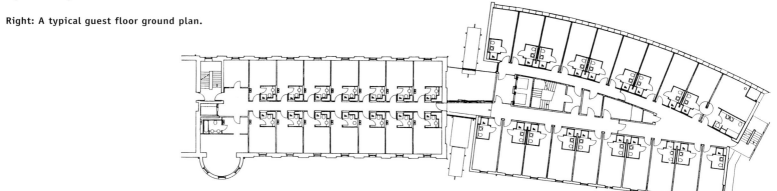

Above right: The Persius Suite is situated in the Grain silo.

Right: Seating and other lobby furnishings were designed by Jasper Morrison.

The Metropolitan

London, Great Britain, 1997

Architecture: Mark Pinney Associates

Interior Design: United Designers

LONDON'S most famous hotel district on Park Lane has not changed substantially for decades. Here, such quintessentially British establishments as The Dorchester and Grosvenor House line up alongside the international mainstream, including the Hilton, Four Seasons and Intercontinental hotels. A prime spot, if perhaps rather unexciting. Until the beginning of 1997, that is, when The Metropolitan opened its doors and immediately became the most fashionable hotel in the British capital. No-one could have foreseen such a glittering future for this plain 1960s building, which formerly led a rather dismal existence amidst its more famous neighbours, going under the distinctly unglamorous name of the Londonderry Hotel. The building might have been demolished altogether: after all, this prime West End plot was clearly yielding nothing like its proper value. However, Singapore-born entrepreneur Christina Ong, who had already established a successful chain of fashion stores in England, decided otherwise. Swinging London was once again setting the style in fashion and music: she wanted to give the city a designer hotel to match.

The intimate Halkin Hotel, which she had operated since 1991, had initiated her in the arts of pampering guests from the art and fashion worlds. Yet here the scale of the enterprise was altogether larger. Ong engaged United Designers, a group that had achieved

fame with the Conran restaurant projects in London and the Clarence Hotel in Dublin, built a new wing and invested £45 million in the project. 'The hotel has gone up a couple of stars since we started. It's fresh, contemporary and fun. We're trying to make it much more of a venue. We felt that in today's world the most valuable commodity is space and so we wanted to create an air of space – we designed the furniture to be quite light, almost as if it floats,' explained interior designer Keith Hobbs of United Designers.

In total the Metropolitan has more than 12,000 square metres of usable floor space, encompassing 155 rooms and suites along with conference rooms, a health club and restaurants, which are intended to become the fashionable places to meet. In the spacious Met Bar on the ground floor you can rub shoulders with the in-crowd until three in the morning. On the floor above is a branch of the fashionable New York restaurant Nobu – famous not only for its exotic Japanese-Peruvian cuisine but also for having Robert de Niro as one of its shareholders. This marketing mix of sleeping and eating in style is drawing in the rich and famous from far and wide, and establishing the hotel's reputation as a stylish and exclusive venue. In this ideal marriage of functions the restaurant currently has the lead by a whisker, at least as far as staff uniforms are concerned: while the hotel staff have to content themselves with a special collection from Donna Karan's DKNY, the waiters were dressed by Issey Miyake.

Soon the Metropolitan will have a competitor, and it's staying in the family: spurred on by his wife Christina, Singapore tycoon Ong Beng Seng is building London's next designer hotel in the Docklands. When choosing his interior designer he went straight to the top and engaged Philippe Starck, the grand master of hotel design.

Above, right: The plain 1960s building in Park Lane houses the fashionable Metropolitan hotel.

Below: The Nobu restaurant with etched glass panels and oriental style furniture is a branch of a trendy New York company.

The reception area has a specially created
abstract rug by Helen Yardley and
a *bas relief* clock by Complete Fabrication.
Digitally programmed lighting set
above glass panelling produces a natural
daylight effect.

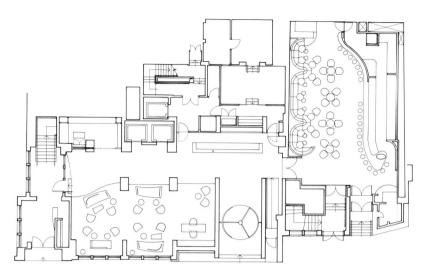

Above: Ground-floor plan.

Right: Sketches of customized furnishing details.

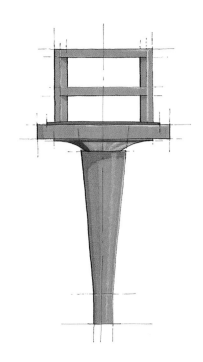

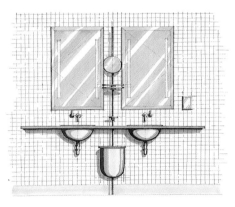

Above: The guest rooms have been designed to be warm and inviting through the use of beautifully fashioned hardwood and a muted palette of natural fabrics.

Left: The bar contributes a separate atmosphere to the rest of the hotel with dark colour ranges and shiny surfaces.

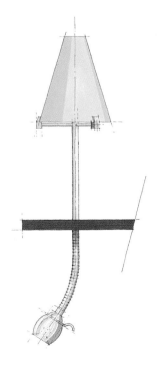

The Clarence Hotel

Dublin, Ireland, 1996

Architecture: Philip O'Reilly, Costello Murray Beaumont

Interior Design: United Designers

THE Clarence Hotel was erected on the left bank of the River Liffey in 1852, and since Temple Bar, the area around it, became the focus of the young artistic scene in Dublin in the 1970s, this magnificent building with its faded splendour has attracted a motley clientele. When the building came up for sale recently, it was snapped up by three Dubliners who regularly frequented its bar. Harry Crosbie, an entrepreneur who made his fortune in the property business (including the now legendary venue The Point), joined forces with rock musicians Bono and The Edge from the Irish mega-band U2 to save both their favourite watering hole and the hotel that housed it. The building needed general renovation, and the trio chose a British team for this: United Designers, whose founder Keith Hobbs achieved early fame as Sir Terence Conran's design partner on the fashionable London restaurants Quaglino's and Mezzo.

The Dubliners gave the Londoners a very strict brief: 'The challenge was to create a contemporary hotel without losing the traditional character. We've left it quite quirky. We could have ironed out and been precise but we didn't want it to be too purist or smart alec. It should be seen as luxurious, but a bit odd too. It's distinctly Irish' (Keith Hobbs). The terracotta façade was carefully restored and a new roof storey was added, matching the style of the original building. In the important public spaces on the ground floor the work was confined to bringing out the original beauty of the existing building. In the Octagon Bar, the bar itself was moved to the centre of the room and covered with a new octagonal glass dome. The Ballroom with its huge Arts and Crafts leaded windows and six-metre-high stucco ceiling became the setting for the restaurant, The Tea Room.

In order to provide the level of comfort that is expected of a five-star hotel, in Ireland as elsewhere, United Designers reduced the number of rooms from its original 70 to the present number of 50. At the top is the new penthouse with its own outdoor roof garden and jacuzzi. Wood panelling predominates on the ground floor, elsewhere the light-coloured walls are complemented with matching warm shades. Much of the furniture and most of the flooring is made of oak. The furnishings were designed by the interior designers, down to the small details, but here, too, they had to follow the directives issued by their Dublin clients: as far as possible, all the craftworkers, manufacturers and materials used to create this splendid new Clarence had to be Irish.

The Client's brief was to update the hotel but keep the atmosphere of the original building.

Opposite, top: The Octagon Bar has open fires and original dark oak wooden panelling.

Opposite, below: The Arts and Crafts leaded windows of the former ballroom have been retained in the restaurant.

Below: The roof top private garden of the newly added penthouse overlooks the river Liffey.

The outdoor penthouse jacuzzi offers splendid privacy under the open Dublin's skies.

The number of guest rooms was reduced from the former 70 to 50 to allow for more spacious and sumptuous accommodation. Touches of cardinal colours have been added to give warmth and maintain traditional Irish flair.

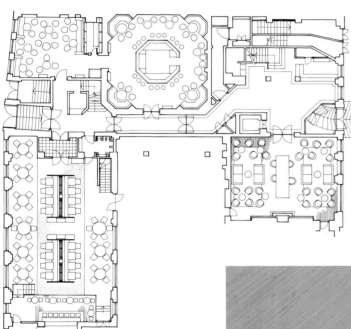

Above: Ground-floor plan

Right: The penthouse uses natural colour tones to complement the wooden detailing of the floor and ceiling.

The Adelphi Hotel

Melbourne, Australia, 1993

Architecture/Interior Design: Denton Corker Marshall

Above: The entrance to the Adelphi at night reveals the careful use of colour accents in the public areas. The exterior of the two lower stories are clad in aluminium tiles.

Right: Perspective of the building showing the tight street front with projecting roof-top pool.

A WAREHOUSE dating from 1938, standing in the heart of Melbourne, eight metres wide along the street front and 48 metres deep. This was the crude structural base from which Melbourne architects Denton Corker Marshall fashioned a new trend-setting hotel for the South Australian city: 'The design for the Adelphi is based on the premise of minimizing the amount of change to the external fabric and structure of the existing building. This was partly dictated for reasons of cost, but also to clarify the juxtaposition of old and new. The aim was not to transform the building through extensive reshaping and remodelling, but via the addition of new elements and components.' Their alterations produced a radical design which draws force from the contrast between the rough commercial architecture of the past and the very different colours and materials of the contemporary additions.

Old and new are set in counterpoint, from the bistro in the basement, through the lobby with bar on the upper ground floor and the six floors of guest rooms, culminating in a gesture of grand simplicity with three new storeys added on top of the original eight. In the penthouse is a private members' club frequented by Melbourne's cultural élite and a 25-metre swimming pool. The glazed end of the pool sticks out in the air, high above Flinders Lane: a delightful architectural joke which is enough in itself to make the Adelphi a modern place of pilgrimage. Yet the rest of the hotel, with its 34 rooms and suites and a total area of 3,217 square metres, by no means lags behind this dizzying, rooftop swimming experience. The limited budget of $4 million did not cramp the designers' style in the slightest: on the contrary, it fuelled their strictly minimalist approach.

Denton Corker Marshall were responsible for all the interior design. In the upper storeys, the guest rooms are all placed on the longer side of the building; the architects decorated the corridors with impressive examples of contemporary Australian photography. However, anyone expecting the Adelphi to market itself, in minimalist fashion, as an ascetic budget hotel will be disappointed. For all the sparseness of the décor, the hotel claims five star status: it is targeted at style-conscious globetrotters who are tired of the mainstream luxury of the top international hotels. Now it seems that the latest status symbol is to pay more for less: asceticism is the hallmark of the élite.

The roof-top, cantilevered swimming pool with glass bottom
is suspended over the busy Flinders Lane.

Above: The bedrooms are sparse and angular. The geometric abstract shapes in acid hues, which form the back of the plain leather chaise, act as a colourful foil to the austere futon-like beds and black floors.

Right, top: Typical guest room floor and, below, level 10 with the pool deck and club bar.

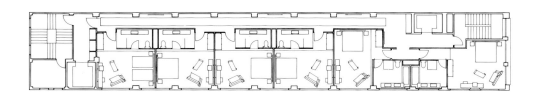

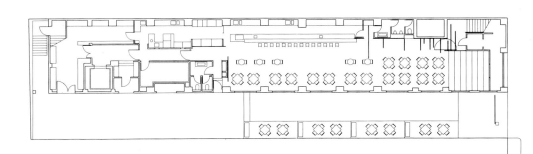

Above: The basement café has a clear-sealed granolithic concrete floor, aluminium walls and bars.

Below: Sketches of the bistro chairs designed by Denton Corker Marshall.

The roof extension with club area and pool deck is housed in a black-stained concrete structure infilled with glass, galvanized steel or brightly coloured metal panels.

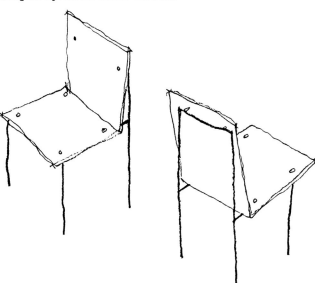

Point Hotel

Edinburgh, Great Britain, 1995-7

Architecture/Interior Design: Andrew Doolan Architects

'GREAT architecture created by very direct means, an object lesson for fussy hoteliers,' enthused Scotland's Royal Incorporation of Architects when the Point Hotel was awarded one of its highly-regarded Regeneration Design Awards in 1996. The 'regeneration' carried out by Edinburgh team Andrew Doolan Architects affected a substantial corner plot in the city. Andrew Doolan, architect and owner of the property company Kantel, purchased the department store in 1994 after the building had lain empty from 1987, and his company now owns and manages the hotel. The outside of the building, constructed on an iron-shaped ground plan in 1914, had survived the years relatively unscathed; inside barely anything of the historical structure remained. The architects decided to gut the building and restructure it completely. 'The concept behind the hotel was simple – to provide reasonably priced bedroom accommodation above a ground floor bar-restaurant in a contemporary manner, of a standard appropriate to a capital city. The foyer illustrates the minimal approach to interior design throughout the hotel, relying on sharp detailing, bold colours and dramatic lighting combined with a general lack of clutter' (Andrew Doolan, architect and owner).

The architects created a display-window frontage, opening up new perspectives which were effectively incorporated into the interior design. The hotel entrance is beautifully designed: a yellow wall sweeps impressively through the lobby to the reception, while bare neon tubes glow in bright colours, a reference to Dan Flavin's light works. The café-restaurant features chandeliers modelled on those in the Obecní Dum in Prague. A meeting room is located behind the large arched windows of the mezzanine, and there are 55 rooms in the five upper storeys.

The second stage of the project, completed in 1997, incorporated a neighbouring building, bringing the total number of rooms to 100. A third phase is underway, which will bring the number of rooms to 130 and will incorporate an external courtyard to the rear, a conference centre, leisure facilities and car parking. Most rooms offer picture-postcard views over the city and its castle. The rooms are furnished in line with the architects' credo: nothing superfluous, but everything that is necessary to make the guests feel comfortable. The traditional furniture creates a pleasant atmosphere of moderation and restraint. Yet there is no trace of any overstrained purism here: just the very best in four-star comfort.

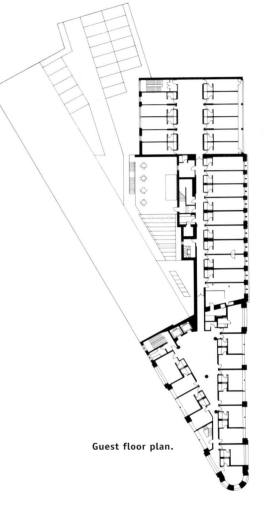

Guest floor plan.

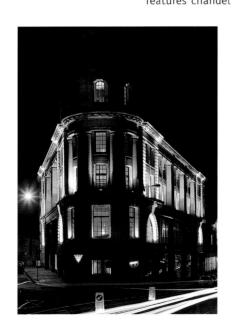

Left: Night shot of the entrance. Conference facilities are located behind the massive arched windows on the first floor.

Right: The Upper Lobby is a perfectly wrought example of minimalist design relying on careful detailing, bold lighting effects and strong colours.

Left: Lounge area with curved wall leading to reception.

Below: The simple, elegant design of the double sized jacuzzi is enlivened by underwater lights and a fluorescent wall.

Opposite: The restaurant is subdivided into sections to afford a degree of privacy for diners. The Art Deco chandeliers are based on a Czech design for the Obecní Dum in Prague.

Bleibtreu Hotel

Berlin, Germany, 1995

Architecture: Werner Weitz

Interior Design: Herbert Jacob Weinand

THE Bleibtreu Hotel, located close to the Kurfürstendamm in west Berlin, opened its doors in 1995 and has already become an architectural classic. More than any other building, this converted Wilhelminian apartment block embodies the ideology and practice of the young German design rebels. 'Living off the wall': this was the slogan coined by these representatives of the New Design movement in the 1980s, in their campaign for the rejection of industrialization and for the re-emotionalization of everyday objects. Herbert Jacob Weinand was one of the movement's key figures in Berlin, active as an instigator, a participant and a gallery owner. The commission to design the complete interior of the new hotel in the Bleibtreustraße gave him a belated opportunity to display his talents. His client, the owner of the small Savoy hotel group, knew what she was in for: Weinand had designed the interior of her private residence not long before.

The Bleibtreu Hotel was converted into a thoroughly idiosyncratic Berlin amalgam at a cost of DM18 million. It celebrates that boisterous artistic movement, while at the same time maintaining a critical distance; it quotes motifs from Prussian forebears such as Schinkel, yet expresses an irrepressible longing for more southern climes. The style of the architecture is firmly rooted in more recent traditions; homeliness and decorative simplicity are combined with a sense of ecological mission, while the lavish use of mosaics creates an impression of mediterranean flair. 'We wanted to create a realm of experience very different from the usual hotel business, a place of aesthetic enjoyment and sensuous experience which offers the guest calm, relaxation and stimulation at the same time. In Hotel Bleibtreu this complexity is expressed through the interplay of design and art' (Herbert Jacob Weinand).

The design of the entrance area displays both wit and intelligence: here the guests become passers-by, walking past the shop fronts of a delicatessen and a florist. On their way through to reception, at the rear of the building, they can choose between the lively espresso café with its adjoining Blue Bar and restaurant, or a passageway leading directly into a small, immaculate inner courtyard with a striking 12-metre-long ceramic table.

The four-star hotel has 60 rooms and a health club in the basement. Weinand's design is also environmentally aware: the furnishings were produced and installed as far as possible without the use of toxic chemicals; natural dyes and pure wool carpets were used; furniture and parquet floors were treated with oil rather than varnish. Organic and natural products predominate in the delicatessen and on the restaurant menu. The Bleibtreu Hotel is also designed to spoil its guests in more subtle ways, with a little New-Age mysticism: cupboard handles made of jasper conduct positive energies, while the lighting and ventilation systems have been fine-tuned to stimulate the senses. And of course the health club offers not only the conventional steam baths and massage but also Bach flower remedies, colour therapy and aromatherapy.

Right: The hotel is located in a *fin de siècle* apartment block close to the Kurfürstendamm in Berlin.

Opposite, top: Through a passageway guests reach the courtyard where a 12-metre-long communal dining table in blue mosaic designed by Andreas Tesch invites you to socialize.

Opposite, bottom: ground-floor plan.

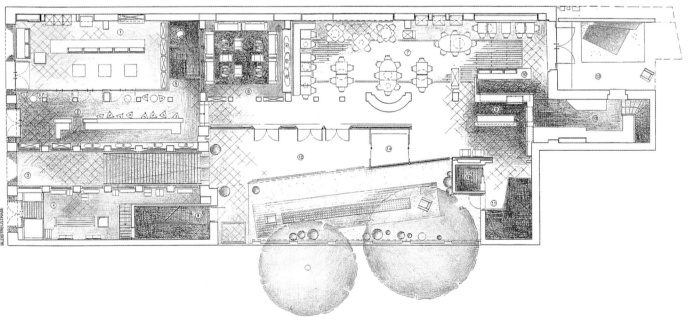

The restaurant has lamps in Murano Glass designed by Atelier Weinand. The predominantly white décor is soft and inviting, warmth being added by the generous use of oak detailing and colourful highlights.

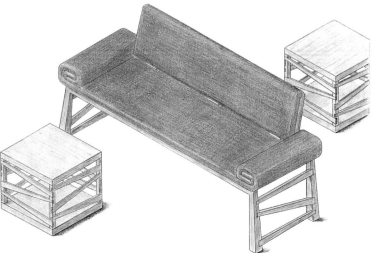

Above: The Blue Bar has specially designed furniture using non toxic materials and dyes and is treated with oil rather than varnish. The carpets are of pure wool.

Left: Sketches of bar furnishing details.

Idiosyncratic artistic details such as Rosemarie Sansonetti's *Sedia Alte* (1993) are placed throughout the hotel.

Right: The bedrooms use customized furnishings designed by Weinand and supplied by Porro Industria Mobili. Each floor is given an individual character by the use of different colours. On the top floor contrasting stripes and patterns have been selected to create a contemporary 'Schinkel' effect.

The bathrooms are enlivened by the use of brightly coloured, glazed tiles.

Hotel La Pérouse

Nantes, France, 1993

Architecture/Interior Design: Barto + Barto

Above: The stone-faced, modernist design of the hotel nevertheless respects the roof height of this historic site in the centre of Nantes.

Right: Section view of the hotel.

Opposite: The absence of colour enforces the effect of natural wood in the stairwell leading to the guest floors.

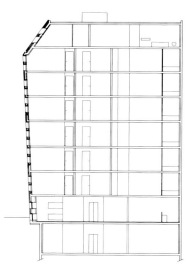

THIS uncompromising minimalist monument created by local architects Bernard and Clotilde Barto stands amidst protected buildings in the historic centre of Nantes. With its white stone facing and its strictly geometrical windows the Hotel La Pérouse provides a forceful contrast with its eminent neighbours, while at the same time conforming to its surroundings in terms of eave height, façade structure and building outline. The design's inherent tension between tradition and modernism is unmistakable, and this concept was at the heart of the architects' design philosophy from the outset: 'Building in an urban context means resisting the easy option of ready-made solutions. It means responding to the character of old town centres. We all imagine heavy, reassuring, opulent buildings: how can we achieve the presence, the materiality of the old buildings while using modern methods of construction? By using minimalist methods, applied in exactly the right place. A project like this takes a stand, it is not silent. It makes use of the designers' capacity to bring extremes to life' (Barto + Barto). Here the strategy of contrasts and correspondences has produced a coherent architectural style. The closed body of the building is offset by the gleaming white of the stone facing. The window slits embedded in it provide a clever connection between the old five-storey building which shares the same plot and the seven storeys of the new three-star hotel.

La Pérouse has a total floor space of 1,258 square metres and 48 rooms which echo the austere style of the architecture. There is no colour here: the only variations from the pure white asceticism are the black blinds on the windows and the wood of the floors, stairways and furniture. Glass cupboards in the rooms and glass washbasins in the bathrooms contribute to the purist approach of the whole. The architects designed this spartan interior themselves, with the exception of a few pieces by classic modernist designers like Eileen Grey and Gerrit Rietveld. They have no dogmatic ideas as to the effect their strict design is intended to have on the hotel guests. However, entering this minimalist stage set may enhance the shock of the outer form

Just as the building fulfils a cathartic role in the urban context, so the monastic sparseness of the interior has a uniquely therapeutic effect. This is not so surprising when you learn that Clotilde Barto once studied psychopathology.

The clear cut design of the reception area is dominated by the oblong window slits mirrored by Eileen Grey sofas especially chosen for their horizontality.

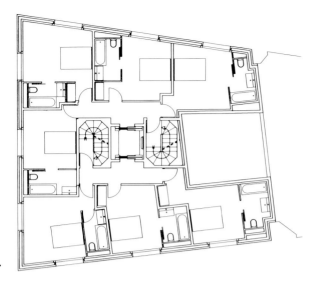

Typical guest room floor plan.

The dining room has the atmosphere of
a monastic refectory.

Glass wardrobes in the guest rooms
and angular furnishings are major
elements of the spartan interior design.

Rogner-Bad Blumau

Blumau, Austria, 1997

Architecture: Friedensreich Hundertwasser, Peter Pelikan

Interior Design: Friedensreich Hundertwasser

FRIEDENSREICH HUNDERTWASSER was always the most unruly of the Viennese late surrealists. For him it was not enough just to produce fantastical paintings: he was involved in artistic-political campaigns and pleaded vociferously for a return to nature at a time when most of his contemporaries could not even spell the word 'ecology'. And now, while others are still talking about eco-friendly, energy-efficient buildings, Hundertwasser has created his own colourful style of architecture, working towards a new, enduring harmony between function and style. He has already supplied tangible evidence of his theories, with residential buildings in Vienna and elsewhere, a children's nursery in Frankfurt, even a power station in Austria. However, his largest project yet – and his most expensive, with a budget of DM140 million – is a spa building in the Steiermark region: the Rogner-Bad Blumau, a hotel with thermal baths which nestles into the undulating landscape with its brightly coloured patterns and its organic, playful shapes, looking for all the world as if a Hundertwasser painting had just come to life.

Grass, bushes and trees grow on the roofs of the building. The façades bear relief compositions of plaster, bricks and glass tiles, while the wonderfully amorphous buildings are crowned with turrets, golden domes and battlements. No two windows are the same, and the dimensions of the 247 rooms are similarly diverse. The meandering open-air thermal baths and the indoor bath and spa facilities are open to the public, not just to hotel guests. Many people come for the day and are astonished to see how imaginative, entertaining and natural contemporary architecture can be. Hundertwasser sees his Blumau fairyland as a declaration of war on his élitist profession: 'Modern architecture is designed for computers and machines; people are in the way in it, let alone nature. People are just guinea pigs for perverse architectural or educational experiments. There is no point designing a building with the very latest in ecological technologies if it is hideously ugly at the same time. Ecology must not just go down the industrial path: it must also be beautiful and creative in order to function'.

Yet the architecture of Rogner-Bad Blumau is also intended to be experimental in a human, environmentally-friendly way: the roofs (which Hundertwasser calls 'rolling hills') of the two elongated buildings rise up gently from the landscape, providing viewpoints and walking areas, while their covering of earth and plants insulates the floors beneath from heat in the summer and from cold in the winter, produces oxygen, reduces pollutants and filters rainwater. And experiencing Hundertwasser's colourful world is surely also an educational experience, although again in a very different way. The beautifully modulated irregularity, the deliberate avoidance of norms and sterile uniformity goes so far that even the floors are intentionally uneven, to stimulate an awareness of balance: 'The winding arcade with the uneven floor becomes a symphony, a melody for the feet, and brings back natural vibrations to man' (Hundertwasser).

Above: The thermal pool area of Rogner-Bad Blumau is surrounded by a surreal architectural fantasy landscape.

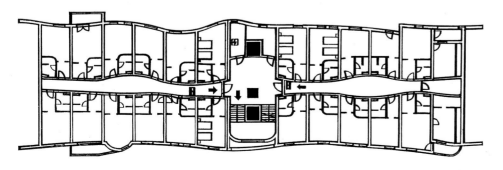

Left: Guest room floor plan of the main building.

Opposite: Detail of a joyfully coloured ceramic column.

THERMALWASSER
THERMAL WATER
ca. 36°
BADEZEIT
BATHING TIME
max. 20 min.

Opposite: Amorphous sculptured bathroom on a guest floor.

Right: The restaurant area.

The concept of irregularity based on an artistic order of patterns and colours turns the façades into picturesque paintings.

new business hotels

The mundane sphere of the business world, where for decades stopovers, meetings and conferences took place in drab, purely functional settings, is currently increasing in value. In the office world, architecture re-established its primacy by responding to the need for new architectural corporate identities following the virtualization of work processes and company structures. Now this development is also affecting business hotels. A series of exemplary projects have been created, many of them created by internationally renowned architects' offices, inspired and influenced by the success of the design hotels. In some cases there have been fruitful collaborations with protagonists of innovative hotel design, like Andrée Putman. Yet, for all the stylistic pluralism, objectivity and austerity of form still prevail. The change of aesthetic values has 'neutralized' the self image and ambitions of the globally active economic élite and so given rise to its suitable architectural expression. Appropriately enough, many of these new business hotels have been created in the context of renovation projects for disused industrial sites.

Seidler Hotel Pelikan

Hanover, Germany, 1995

Architecture: Dieter Neikes

Interior Design: Harald Klein, Aut-Design

GREEN and black Pelikan fountain pens are still a status symbol among connoisseurs. However, time long since ran out for the Hanover-based firm that manufactured them, and when the company was closed down its historic factory buildings came onto the market. Fortunately this listed industrial ensemble, built between 1904 and 1906, was saved by an exemplary conversion project. The new Pelikan complex, designed by architect Dieter Neikes to revitalize the historic site, opens up the former factory for a variety of uses: offices and surgeries, a sport and therapy centre, homes and restaurants are combined in a lively mix of functions.

At the heart of the project is the Seidler Hotel Pelikan with 139 rooms, a banqueting hall, restaurants and the officially licensed Harry's New York Bar. On the outside, the traditional red brick façade with its green

windows has been impeccably restored, while the interior displays a successful mixture of contemporary styles. The interior was designed by Harald Klein in an eclectic and theatrical fashion: rather than seeking to disguise his borrowings Klein skilfully reworks motifs taken from leading international designers like Philippe Starck and Massimo Iosa-Ghini: 'The design concept acknowledges the industrial architecture, while also preserving a distance from it, with the aim of emotionalizing it in an objective way' (Klein).

The rooms of this former production site were far higher than the conventional dimensions of hotel rooms, but Klein adhered to his design principle and did not disguise this in the conventional way (by adding a suspended ceiling) but rather highlighted and transformed it through the use of translucent textiles, hung across the room as a kind of vaulting. The bold colours of the walls make a pleasant change from the widespread obsession with transforming disused commercial buildings into bland, whitewashed anonymity. The high point of the project is the hotel bar, located in the narrow front of a multi-purpose hall opposite the hotel entrance. It is scarcely as wide as a handkerchief but tremendously high, with a monumental counter across its entire width which triumphantly defies all the constrictions of the site and the ground plan.

For Hanover, a town with a long tradition of exhibitions and the host for EXPO 2000, the successful conversion of the Pelikan site is an important step towards its post-industrial future. In the run-up to this millennial event it was no coincidence that the Seidler Hotel Pelikan was chosen as the venue for launching the EXPO mascot, created by Spanish designer Javier Mariscal as a lucky emblem for the town and the region.

A former courtyard of the Pelikan Fountain Pen Factory became the glazed driveway between the hotel entrance and Harry's New York Bar.

Preceding pages: Harry's New York Bar is positioned in the front of a multi-purpose hall. The exceptionally narrow but very high space is dominated by a huge counter and a gilded wall across its entire width.

Left: The lobby lounge with coffee bar at rear.

Opposite: A guest room with translucent fabric vaulted ceiling, customized furniture and settee by Massimo Iosa-Ghini.

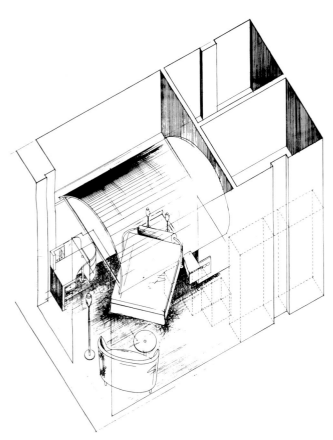

Above: Axonometric view of a typical guest room.

Right: Three-seater sofas in glitzy silver fabric highlight parts of the lobby.

Sheraton Paris Airport Hotel

Roissy, France, 1996

Architecture: Paul Andreu/Martinet Architecture

Interior Design: Andrée Putman, ECART

Below: The hotel sits proudly over the TGV station in the middle of Terminal 2 of Roissy Airport.

Opposite: The four-galleried storeys of the guest floors surround a glass atrium whose bottom is part of the station complex ceiling.

TRANSLATING technological progress into architectural symbols seems to be a very French preoccupation. For years the French have dedicated themselves to the pursuit of ever-faster traffic flows on land and in the air, and to the perfect networking of high-speed trains and planes – and these technological achievements have found their counterparts in high-tech architectural metaphors. First there was Lyon, where the TGV trains arrive in Santiago Calatrava's breathtaking station design at Satolas airport. Now the latest techno-architectural masterpiece can be admired at Roissy, in Terminal 2 of the Charles de Gaulle airport. Elsewhere railways may be regarded as a mere service function and hidden away in dark concrete shafts; here the train station is a huge, intricate structure with tall, arching glass roofs. Architect Paul Andreu highlights this intersection of different modes of transport as a focal point of our mobile society and reinforces the symbolism by setting a hotel complex directly above the TGV station where it floats like a ship's hull, surrounded by a sea of approach tracks.

This exposed location in the middle of one of Europe's busiest airports, above the constant to-and-fro of local and express trains, made it necessary to have special noise insulation on the façades and the windows, as well as a support structure with a suspension system to eliminate vibration. The futurist outlook of the project proved infectious: the hotel operating company, ITT Sheraton, commissioned Andrée Putman, the *grande dame* of contemporary hotel design, to design the interior of the Sheraton Paris Airport Hotel. For Putman this was an opportunity to continue, for one of the world's leading hotel groups, what she had started twelve years earlier in her exemplary New York hotel Morgans and continued with designs like the Wasserturm Hotel in Cologne: the project of setting definitive standards for contemporary hotel design. 'Our objective has been to create a spirit and an architectural mood which answer to the idea of the hotel at the end of this century: comfortable, functional, timeless and different from the others' (Putman).

The vertical division of the five hotel levels is extremely simple: above the entrance hall with its reception, lobby, Brasserie Les Saisons, Restaurant Les Etoiles and bar are four galleried storeys set along a glazed central atrium, with a total of 265 rooms and suites. The central entrances, lifts and staircases are concealed in a back-lit streamlined unit which runs through the whole foyer area. The design of the internal walkways is governed by the theme of immateriality: curved galleries bordered with glass balustrades open up confusing perspectives; everything is made of glass, not only the atrium roof but also parts of the floor on the entrance level. Set against this cool, impersonal context, the materials and colours which are used in the hotel appear all the more striking and homely: oak doors with slatted panels, cherrywood furniture, sand-coloured furniture in the rooms, carrara marble in the bathrooms. These and many other carefully chosen, user-friendly details combine to create a hotel that is indeed 'different from the others', just as Andrée Putman wanted.

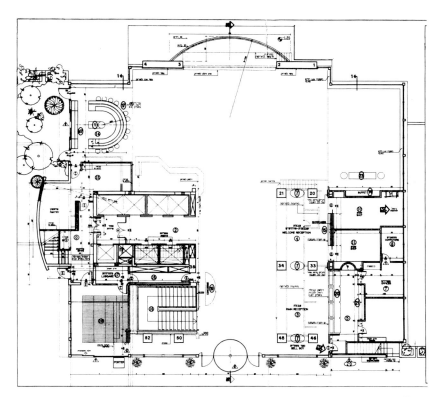

Plan of the ground floor.

Left: Antique furnishings sit happily together with trendy lighting objects by the young Israeli designer Ayala Sperling Serfati.

Below: In the reception area the floors are of Zifchah slate and the desk is covered with zinc and brass.

Hyatt Regency

Fukuoka, Japan, 1993

Architecture/Interior Design: Michael Graves

SINCE the late 1980s Fukuoka has been a fertile location for the top international architects: leading contemporary designers have carried out a large number of projects here. America's doyen of postmodernism, Michael Graves, has also made a contribution to the new image of this southern Japanese metropolis. The complex he designed, which covers more than 43,000 square metres and cost more than $80 million, is called the Sphinx Center, a name that suits the dual character of this impressive building: a Hyatt Regency Hotel with 260 rooms is combined with two office blocks in an attractive functional mix. 'The client wanted to create a business hotel that would support an attached site use despite strict zoning controls' (Michael Graves).

The small plot that was available between a public park on one side and a river on the other meant that the building had to be very compact, yet the architect's expert gradation of the different sections ensures that there is no feeling of heaviness. Facing the park Graves opened up a *cour d'honneur* as the approach to the central hotel rotunda, which is flanked by two six-storey wings. The rotunda with its four copper-faced circles of pillars towers over the forebuilding and conceals the rather plain, eleven-storey office block behind it. At the far end of the site is the low ballroom pavilion with its barrel roof, bordering the rather cheerless riverbank.

Here, as in other projects, Graves uses one of his favourite 'pop classical' effects: a round atrium bordered with colonnades. However, this time the pillars do not soar right up to the roof: they are topped with a pyramid, a copper-covered piece of architectural sculpture, which fills the space of the empty cylinder above the seventh floor of the 13-storey rotunda. And, as if Graves could not resist the motif, the round form is repeated twice in the next, square-shaped, atrium, where there is a golden staircase temple. This forms the perfect backdrop for photographs of newly-married couples, because wedding chapels are a standard facility offered by Japanese luxury business hotels.

As previously with the Hyatt Regency in La Jolla, California, the architect was also commissioned to produce much of the interior decoration. All the public spaces and the guest rooms bear his imprint, right down to the furniture and lights. Graves provided a magisterial solution for the client's requirement that ordinary guest room functions should be optimized: the furniture he designed allows the rooms to be converted for use as an office or conference room, and the number of beds can be increased to accommodate four or five people. Thus each room in the Hyatt Regency echoes in miniature the synthesis of working and sleeping which characterizes the Sphinx Center as a whole.

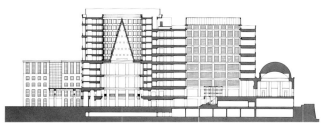

Left: The Sphinx Centre covers 43,000 square metres of downtown Fukuoka and houses offices as well as the Hyatt Regency Hotel.

Above: A longitudinal section.

Opposite: The golden rotunda in the second hotel atrium court.

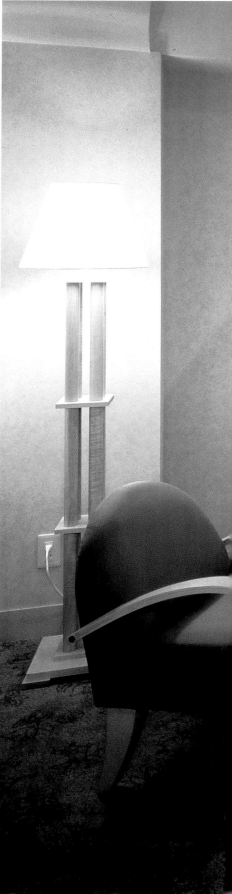

Right: Michael Graves was also responsible for the interior furnishings of the various types of guest rooms.

Above: The pyramid which covers the first circular atrium is clad in copper and rises through the cylinder of the central tower and can be viewed as an architectural sculpture from the guest room corridors.

Below: Ground-floor plan.

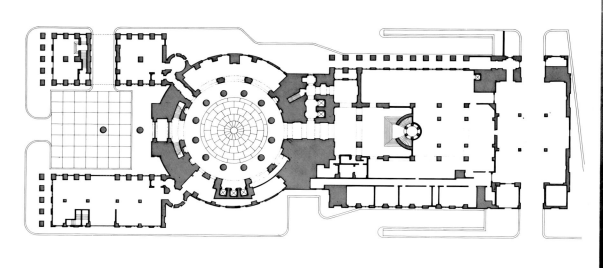

Le Méridien Lingotto

Turin, Italy, 1995

Architecture: Renzo Piano Building Workshop

Interior Design: Franco Mirenzi, Unimark

THE massive Turin car factory, dating from 1920, is a unique example of early twentieth-century industrial architecture. This impressive monumental building by architect Giacomo Matte-Trucco looks like a Futurist manifesto set in concrete. With the Lingotto factory, Fiat ushered in the age of mass car production in Italy. The assembly process began on the ground floor and continued on the upper storeys; the test track for new cars was on the roof of the huge complex. Yet all the Futurist optimism of the architecture was no guarantee against the passing of time: technical progress and profitability constraints finally made what had once been the pride of the company into an obsolete encumbrance.

Company patriarch Giovanni Agnelli did not want to part with the disused building, however, and he organized a competition among internationally renowned architects. The eventual winner was fairly close at hand: Renzo Piano of Genoa, who presented a design with a mix of functions. 'The idea is to create a city within the city. Like ancient Roman towns this one starts with a simple grid, you penetrate the mass of the building and then you find unexpected things – he concert hall, the bubble, a shopping street, piazzas.' And a four-star hotel with its own private garden.

Le Méridien Lingotto opened in 1995, its 244 rooms and suites spread over two three-storey wings which are connected by a glass corridor crossing an internal courtyard planted with luxuriant subtropical greenery. On the ground floor, alongside the reception and lobby, are the restaurant Le Rivoli and the Garden Bar. Corridors lead to the conference and exhibition centre; lifts give access to the 'bubble' hemisphere on the roof. This extraordinary conference room, built by the brilliant British artist-engineer Peter Rice, formed a striking backdrop for the Turin summit of European heads of government.

The hotel's 22,000 square metres represent only a fragment of the total floorspace of this revitalized industrial site, which is being developed in stages by Piano. The project started with the exhibition area in 1992; the conference and concert hall went into operation in 1994, followed by the business centre and the hotel; the transparent spherical roof pavilion, the symbol of the new Lingotto, was completed in 1996. Still more than a quarter of the total (291,000 square metres) awaits development, and some of the 80 business units have still to be leased. Turin University backed out as a potential tenant, but Fiat remained true to its old production site, moving some departments of its headquarters here. A multiplex cinema is due to open soon. Thus Piano has already succeeded in creating the mix of commerce and culture which he was aiming at from the outset. Italy's national radio orchestra has adopted the Lingotto concert hall as its home base. The car factory's revival is displayed as a permanent exhibition: hotel guests can see all the architects' plans in the hall of Le Méridien Lingotto.

Left: The legendary Fiat factory designed by Giacomo Matte-Trucco had its own test racetrack on the roof. Today the new 'bubble' of the conference centre crowns the historic site.

Opposite: The two wings of the hotel are connected by a glass walled corridor over 'The Garden of Wonders', a private courtyard planted with verdant sub-tropical vegetation.

Left: The conference centre is housed in
a cantilevered high-tech structure designed
by artist-engineer Peter Rice.

Below: The ground-floor plan.

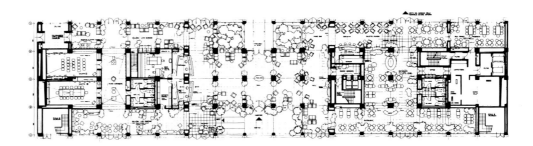

Left: The spacious guest rooms are
comfortably furnished without
bringing to mind the industrial
past of the location.

Opposite: The Lobby has nine-
metre-high ceilings and overlooks
the courtyard. It is decorated with
the original competition entries
of the 20 international architects
who were invited to submit
ideas for the remodelling of the
old factory in 1982.

Soho Grand

New York, USA, 1996

Architecture: Helpern Architects

Interior Design: Studio Sofield

UNTIL recently, SoHo's rise as the artistic and creative epicentre of Manhattan seemed to have bypassed the southern corner of the district, where West Broadway and Grand Street meet. This all changed at a stroke with the opening of the SoHo Grand. The advent of this hotel, which looks as if it had always been there, set in motion the rapid gentrification of a district once dominated by light industry and commercial lots. The new structure, with its 16 tapering storeys, stands head and shoulders above the older buildings around it, presenting a model example of the backward-looking trend in American design that first appeared in Ralph Lauren's fashion designs.

William Sofield, who was commissioned to design the interiors of the Soho Grand, had previously produced grand retro-style shop designs for Lauren's fashion empire; here the client Emanuel Stern had similar aims in mind: 'I wanted a Victorian, turn-of-the-century hotel that met what SoHo is today'. The architecture, designed by Helpern Architects, conforms to the stylistic register of the building's surroundings. The façade is straightforward and unornamented, matching the old industrial buildings around it. The materials used are also traditional: brick walls with bands of stone, cast iron and wood. Planning orders stipulated that the ground floor should be reserved for sales purposes, with the hotel beginning only above this level. This resulted in a modest entrance and a first floor that is all the more impressive by contrast.

Studio Sofield's design turns the arrival into a journey to the past: 'Our premise was to interpret the best of SoHo from 1870 to 1970, reclaiming other spaces but not just recreating elements. We felt compelled to react to SoHo's evolution from an obscure industrial section of the city into what is arguably one of the world's most trendy and exclusive destinations'. The design recreates the Art Déco atmosphere of a New York city hotel from the 1930s, with a few discordant elements thrown in. It also follows its historical model in opting for measured practicality rather than high-class opulence. The lounge is crammed with old-fashioned furniture, while the design of the Grand Bar and the Canal House restaurant is agreeably sparse and conventional. There is no overblown showiness anywhere, not even in the 369 rooms and the four penthouse suites. In place of the customary, built-in furniture the rooms have a traditional ensemble of free-standing pieces: cupboard, chest of drawers, bedside tables, all specially designed for the building. With a few exceptions the art works on display in the SoHo Grand also stick to past grandeur: vintage photographs by Berenice Abbot, Arthur Leipzig and Harold Roth show historic scenes of life in New York.

Right: The retro style brick building sits on the corner of West Broadway and Grand Street.

Opposite: The giant cast iron and bottle glass staircase leads to the reception desk on the first floor.

Preceding pages: The Grand bar (left) quotes the flair of Thirties period New York hotels. Large-scale photo prints of Manhattan's past flank the walls in the lobby stairwell (right) and other areas.

Left: A guest room interior with free standing classic furniture and prevailing sombre tones.

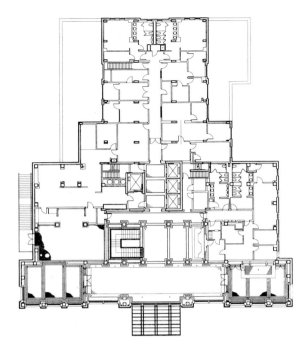

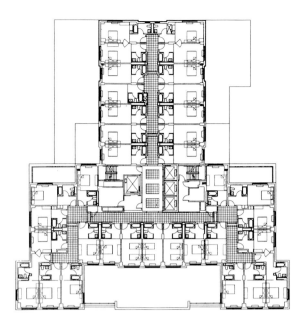

Above: Ground-floor plan (left); guest
floor plan (right)

Living room in one of the suites
with custom-made furniture
designed by Studio Sofield in a
restrained neo-déco manner.

Hotel Kyocera

Kagoshima, Japan, 1995

Architecture/Interior Design: Kisho Kurokawa

IN founding the technopolis of Kokubu Hayato, the Japanese town of Kagoshima is looking to move decisively into the information age. This new area for the high-tech industries of the future is being built near the airport, and its business hotel Kyocera, which covers a floorspace of 25,500 square metres, is designed to meet the needs of both international customers and local companies. Kisho Kurokawa's design is a partly transparent, geometrical architectural sculpture. On an oval ground plan, two curved, thirteen-storey concrete wings surround the glazed central section, which is 60 metres high and undivided by internal struts. The front of the central section looks out over Kinko bay.

The lobby on the ground floor is the focal point of the hotel, leading to the conference centre (in the two-storey basement) and to the first floor which is decked out for weddings and other festive occasions. The understated dignity of this mezzanine – 'zen'-style minimalism meets sleek corporate chic – avoids any suggestion of nostalgic sentimentality. The partygoers are silently transported to the first floor by escalator. In the middle stands the chapel, a rigid glass tent. Architect Kurokawa describes this holy place in rather ambivalent terms: 'This symbolizes the owner's concept of a hotel that is surrounded with love. At the centre of the stained glass, designed with a cross motif, shines a crescent vert ruby, a recrystallized jewel which represents the epitome of groove technology'.

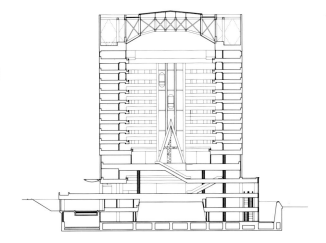

On the floor above this, the hotel offers more worldly, down-to-earth pleasures in its restaurants and bars. The hallways outside the rooms are designed as galleries, offering impressive views of the atrium and the surrounding landscape. On the top floor is the Top Lounge, along with a bar and a meeting room. Apart from a few unavoidable sidesteps, the interiors follow the aesthetic austerity of Kurokawa's design, making this building a rare exception and a notable achievement in the context of Japanese hotel design, where a frequently bizzare pot-pourri of styles is the norm.

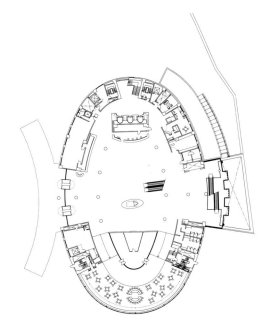

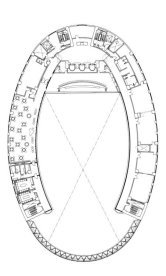

Opposite: The building rises to 60 metres with unparalleled views of the Kirishima Mountains, Sakurajima and Kinko Bay from its transparent curved façade.

Top right: Section showing the two concrete wings surrounding a glazed central atrium.

Left: Thirteenth-floor plan with lounge, bar and boardroom; (far left) first floor plan

Left and below:
Restaurant and bar
areas. The leitmotiv
of the curved wall is
repeated thorughout
the public spaces.

Right: Gallery space on lobby level
one with a solar car display.

Blå Hallen Hotel 11

Göteborg, Sweden, 1993

Architecture: White Arkitekter

Interior Design: White Arkitekter/Margarete & Rolf Åberg/Gunnar Svensson

THE former Eriksberg shipyard is located in the harbour district of Göteborg, which is currently being developed into a new, lively quarter of the city. Among the pioneering projects of this redevelopment scheme was the conversion of a huge industrial building constructed in 1952, where ship's engines were formerly assembled. The huge brick complex (30 metres high and 140 metres long), called Blå Hallen, has become widely known as one of the most successful conversions of disused commercial architecture in Europe. The building houses a lively mix of facilities: a theatre with foyer, Hotel 11 with 133 rooms and suites, a conference centre along with offices and shops, and the Bar-Restaurant 67 on the top floor with views over the Göta Alv quayside. The canopy over the hotel entrance, on one side of the building, stretches over to the neighbouring building, the former engineering workshop, which has been converted into an exhibition gallery.

The architects converted the building without any bogus display of reverence for the industrial architecture: 'We have chosen a policy of working with present-day means of expression for the new elements which are added, and thereby attempt to avoid pastiches. This is in deliberate opposition to the antiquarian viewpoint, which wants to preserve the originality of the buildings, down to the smallest detail. It is important to preserve the overall character and at the same time to add modern changes and a new treatment of details. [To produce something] just as rugged as the original yet not too beautiful or polished, which harbour renewals in other parts of the world might have tended to be. The technical "straight ahead" solutions might be felt to be cold and unveiled to a certain extent. To counteract this mechanistic composition principle, the theatre, bar, breakfast room and hotel entrance have a totally different character of colour, scale and intimacy' (White Arkitekter).

The simple, eye-catching visual language used by the architects owes much to the Dutch De Stijl movement of the 1920s: the blocks of colour and the monumental typography have a straightforward clarity that is perfectly suited to this huge brick building. The architects added a new glass and metal construction, several storeys high, to the roof of the original building. This thoughtful shipyard conversion also encompasses the adjoining open area, where there is car-parking for theatre-goers and hotel guests, along with new facilities for playing tennis, boules and basketball.

Right: The former shipyard complex today houses a theatre, hotel and office facilities.

Opposite: The main atrium rises through the seven floors of the building. The use of bold blocks of colours and strong graphic elements owes much to the De Stijl movement.

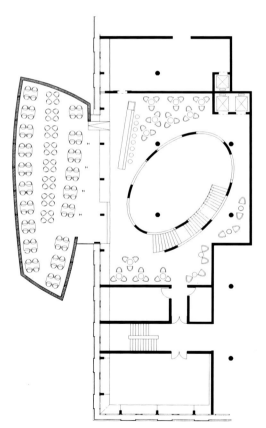

Above: The spacious bedroom of a suite.

Left: The first-floor plan.

Right: The bar gallery surrounds the atrium and has views down into the reception. The artwork is the preliminary study of an installation by Flatz for the Documenta IX exhibition.

PHYSICAL SCULPTURE NO. 5 VORSTUDIE DOCUMENTA IX 1992

Hotel Kempinski Airport

Munich, Germany, 1994

Architecture: Helmut Jahn, Murphy/Jahn

Interior Design: Jan Wichers

THE new Munich airport, at a key European air traffic crossroads, was intended to set new standards in airport design. The greenfield development near the small town of Erding, 50 kilometres from the city, radiates a spirit of revitalized modernism, with its elongated white departure building nestling in former marshland, surrounded by service buildings, freight halls and hangars.

The airport hotel designed by German-American architect Helmut Jahn, with its silvery techno-glamour, provides an effective counterpart to the airport itself. This high-tech hotel is positively revolutionary in the context of the Kempinski Group as a whole, otherwise famous for its tasteful five-star opulence. As with his Paris airport hotel, the Hyatt Regency Roissy, opened two years earlier, Jahn opted for an atrium design. The filigree glass roof construction, 28 metres high at the vertex, stretches across 40 metres between two blocks, each measuring 115 by 20 metres. The atrium is a light-filled piazza crossed by diagonal glass walls and decorated with artificial palms and red armchairs.

The buildings and the surrounding landscape fit together like pieces of a puzzle. The hotel site includes a geometrically designed garden, with car parking spaces underneath it. Entry to the two four-storey wings with the guest rooms is through the atrium lobby. On the floor below this level is the leisure area with the swimming pool, sauna and health club. Pedestrian passageways connect the hotel directly with the airport.

The interior design by Jan Wichers, who previously contributed fairly conservative styles to a few of the Kempinski hotels, also breaks out of the conventional mould. In the design of the restaurant areas Wichers adapts aeronautical motifs, giving them a new twist through his choice of materials. For the lobby he chose contemporary Italian furniture. The furnishings of the 389 rooms manage to be both functional and imaginative in their use of space, while creating an effect of unobtrusive elegance.

The Kempinski Airport Hotel was created as the first stage of a Munich Airport Center (MAC) project planned by Murphy/Jahn, and in design terms it fits seamlessly with the later stages of this business and conference complex. The ornamentation of major air traffic complexes is innately artificial: here this artificiality is turned into a conscious stylistic feature. The artificial nature of the panoply of services which accumulates around the departure and landing area is reflected in the shimmering chic of the architecture.

Left: The hotel wing facing the geometrical formal garden which covers the underground parking.

Opposite: The 28-metre-high glazed atrium area between the two guest room buildings mixes the vocabulary of airport hangars with the escapism of travel.

Left: Open catwalks connect the lift towers in the atrium with the guest floors.

Right: The restaurant area designed by Jan Wichers.

Below: Guest room floor plan.

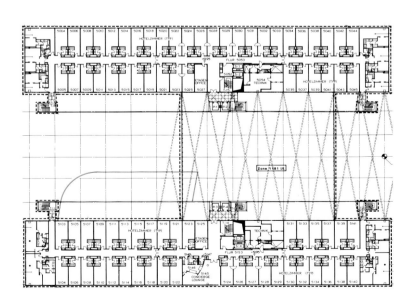

The connecting corridor between the old Kurhaus and the new hotel rotunda.

Right: The façade is made up of horizontal slats of Canadian redwood.

Below: The ground floor plan. The circular building has - except for the underground parking driveway - no entrance of its own and is joined to the old building by a connecting corridor at garden level.

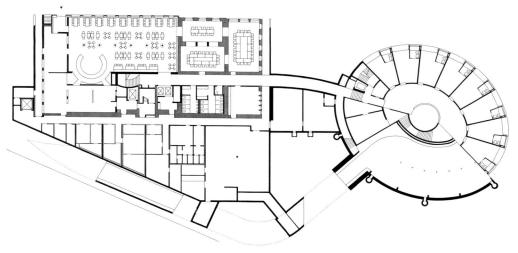

The wedge-shape of the guest rooms allows the bathrooms to be located along the front of the building. All the pieces of furniture are freestanding for a flexible use of space.

Rey Juan Carlos I

Barcelona, Spain, 1992-6

Architecture/Interior Design: Carlos Ferrater/José Maria Cartana

THE 1992 Olympic Games provided an Arabian prince with the perfect pretext for giving Barcelona a brand-new luxury hotel, and this aristocratic investor went straight to the top when naming his new establishment, dedicating it to Spanish king Juan Carlos I. Indeed, since the hotel opened the king has often stayed here on his visits to Barcelona, occupying the royal suite at the top of the hotel, which has a floor space of 700 square metres, a separate lift, and everything a king could ask for in terms of comfort and security. The unique mix of avant-garde design, unconventional architecture and high-quality art has brought Barcelona a new golden age in the 1990s. It may be for this reason that the five-star Hotel Rey Juan Carlos I manages to do without the conventional stylistic fall-backs of high-class kitsch and Arabian Nights exotica.

The hotel, with its 16 storeys and 370 rooms and suites, is designed in a grand, solemn style. From the outside it looks like a luxury modern office block; inside, the construction, built on a prism-shaped ground plan, is surprisingly light and spacious: 'The layout of the building consists of two main wings articulated at the southern end by a 14-storey glazed tower which holds the suites. Inside the dynamic spatial structuring generated by the "sliding" gesture of the polygonal corridors provides an excellent acoustic performance for the great inner void. The folded configuration and horizontal nerves (used as catwalks) of the large glass wall achieve the desired lighting with sparse structural effort' (Ferrater/Cartana).

The magnificent design of the main hall, which is 50 metres high and fully glazed on the north side, is best appreciated from above. The landings with red parquet flooring in the centre of the lobby look as if they have been stacked up haphazardly; in the corners of these asymmetrically arranged squares, oriental carpets neatly mark the position of armchairs and sofas. This impressively designed entrance area leads through to the rooms, the restaurant, and the conference centre housed in the large basement level.

The hotel is located in a newly-built park and leisure area on the edge of the city, close to a main traffic route (the Avenida Diagonal) and surrounded with tennis courts and polo pitches, adding extra attractions to its opulent design. It was intelligent of the architects to change their strategy when they extended the complex in 1996. The health club they added, in the scale and style you would expect of a luxury hotel, was built entirely below ground level. Seven metres under the ground, covered over with grass, is a two-storey spa complex made of bare concrete, with irregularly-shaped rooms grouped around a large star-shaped pool.

Left: The two wings of the hotel are articulated around a 14-storey glazed tower which holds the suites.

Opposite: The atrium rises through the full height of the building. The north wall, entirely of glass, allows natural light to pour into the centre of the building.

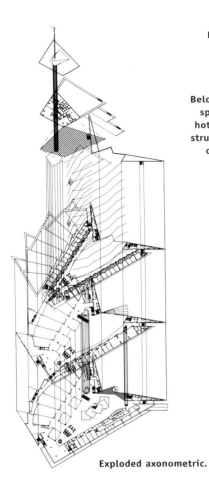

Exploded axonometric.

Right: Bird's eye view down into the hotel reception and lounge area.

Below: The hotel's health spa is built next to the hotel as an underground structure from reinforced concrete and arranged in a star shape.

resort and theme hotels

The outposts of mass tourism have reached right into the furthest corners of the globe. Various marketing strategies have been developed in order to satisfy consumers' hunger for adventure and exoticism. Two segments of the holiday business seem to offer the best prospects for growth, at either end of the spectrum: on the one hand ever more gigantic, immaculately presented fantasy worlds; on the other hand places of retreat that are natural, full of character and supplied with every possible comfort. Fantasies and trivial myths are made into kitsch realities in the vast projects of Las Vegas's entertainment hotels, models of hybrid leisure architecture which have now been exported as far afield as South Africa and Malaysia. At the other end of the scale, ecology is becoming ever more influential. The search for a beautiful, untouched wilderness – though in reality these ecosystems often have to be carefully nurtured in order to survive – revives Rousseauist ideals and harmonizes with the environmental teachings of the green movement. Exemplary instances of thoughtful, minimally invasive resort projects can be found in endangered natural landscapes across the globe, from Africa to the Great Barrier Reef.

Westin Regina Los Cabos Hotel

San Jose del Cabos, Mexico, 1993

Architecture: Sordo Madaleno y Asociados

Interior Design: Division y Diseno de Interiores

ALL over the world there are coastlines that have been disfigured by concrete blocks. Anyone who has seen them will surely believe that tourist facilities should be designed to fit unobtrusively with their context and should be kept to a moderate height. However, the Westin Regina Los Cabos in Baha California, with its flamboyant monumentality, triumphantly neglects these assumptions. This nine-storey ensemble soars up in a bold sweep against the red soil of the rocky peninsula. Geometrically shaped buildings surround meandering pools and sun terraces.

The architects, Sordo Madaleno y Asociados, cite persuasive arguments in defence of their grand gesture: 'We are convinced that this project is determining a new age in hotel design in our country, and all over the world, since it creates a different way of conceptualism setting aside the traditional operating objections that might limit the creativeness of the design. The main concept is to create an oasis or an interior space marked by a large curved wall'. This huge 'wall' is divided into

two and houses the guest rooms, all of which face the sea, while open pergolas run alongside the pool. The reception and conference centre are located in a striking separate block. The restaurant, which faces the beach, forms another annex. Lower units with more guest rooms stand on three terraces on the site.

The total area of this 238-room hotel is 70,000 square metres, and cost more than $138 million to build. A notable feature of the project is the artistic independence that the architects were able to maintain, even working for a hotel group like Westin, which generally seeks to reproduce bland, international designs. The models for Los Cabos are to be found in the best tradition of Mexican modernism – the project has nothing to do with folkloric pastiche with its misconceived imitation of regional culture or a mismatch of local architecture and anonymous five-star conventions. Instead, it displays a confident belief in the symbolic power of architecture, formulating its artistic expression in contrast to its natural setting and so creating its own form of beauty.

The red abstract structure of the resort's main wing forms a dramatic arch that echoes the curve of the beach. All the guest rooms have a view of the sea.

Left: The pool areas are laid out in rounded shapes to match the architectural language of the hotel complex.

Right: Bright colours and the rigid geometry of the structures are magically linked to the elements of water, light, shade and sky.

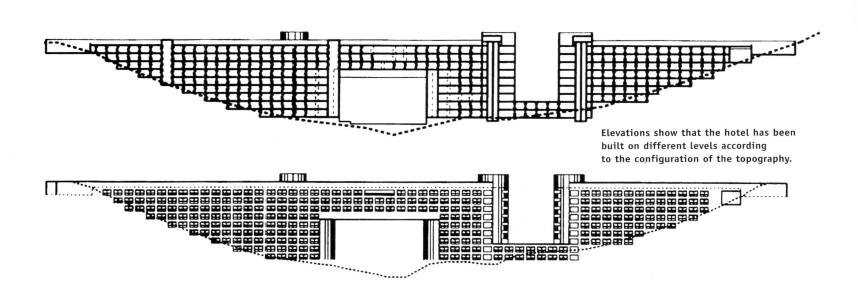

Elevations show that the hotel has been built on different levels according to the configuration of the topography.

Left: This pure and formal architectural sculpture yard faces the hills of the Cero Colorado.

Above: The interiors are finished in sandy colours. The forms evoke traditional Mexican architecture and native art pieces, and cacti have been used as a direct reference to the site.

Below: A site plan showing the relationship of the hotel to the condominium complex

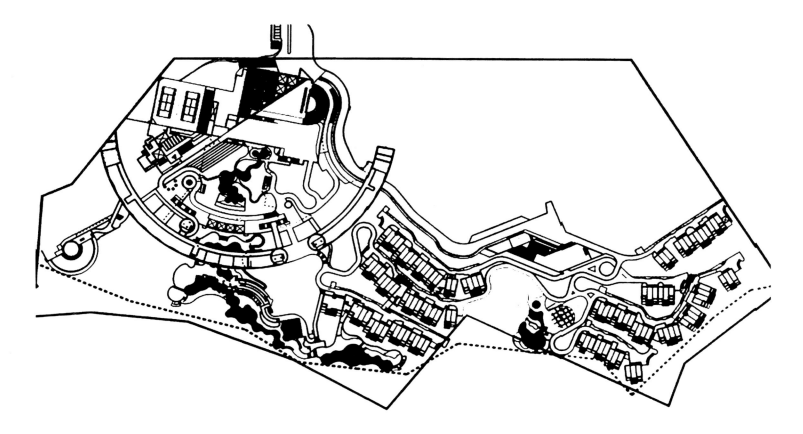

Sea Hawk Hotel and Resort

Fukuoka, Japan, 1995

Architecture: Cesar Pelli & Associates

Interior Designer: Cesar Pelli & Associates/Takanaka Corporation

'THE Sea Hawk Hotel & Resort was planned to be a resort hotel, but in an urban location. The complex forms and patterned surfaces of the exterior and interior draw on associations that are out of the ordinary, and not expected in a large city in Japan. The design reinterprets many traditional components in the imagery of resort hotels, creating a building that offers an escape from daily routine while serving as a good city addition, with careful considerations to its functions, use and neighbouring buildings.' These are the unpretentious words chosen by leading American architect Cesar Pelli to describe one of his most striking Japanese projects. On the sea front in the port town of Fukuoka he has created one of the world's most impressive hotel sites. It also stands right next to the huge baseball stadium, which holds 40,000 spectators and boasts a spectacular mobile roof construction. The scale of the hotel speaks for itself: 1,072 rooms on a useable floor space of more than 138,000 square metres. The sheer class of the architect is apparent in the skill with which he manages the masses of the building, in his combination of abstract constructional volumes with richly-structured façades and roofscapes.

The 36-storey hotel block – a slender oval shape which is flattened off on the land-facing side – refers to the immaculate city skyscrapers that made Pelli famous. In this case, however, the tower block (its neon contours illuminated at night) does not play the central role: it simply provides an appropriate backdrop for the fantasy architecture of the Seahawk Resort itself: a huge glass barrel shape which develops in stages from a cone shape. This glass dome is a palm house, piazza, botanical garden and mock temple rolled into one. The atrium, with its striking rib structure, paraphrases the

mobile stadium roof and thus creates the dimensions that are necessary to ensure that it is not overshadowed by this sporting colossus.

The separation of the public glass plaza and the hotel tower is a concession to the marketing constraints of Japanese hotels. Their profitability depends not only on attracting overnight guests and conference bookings but also on providing a range of on-site entertainments: here, a diverse selection of restaurants and bars, along with a shopping centre, a health club and exotically decorated banquet rooms. Weddings are especially popular here: the happy couples and their guests can enjoy an uninterrupted view over Hakata Bay through the building's impressive glass front. It was here, more than 700 years ago, that an important piece of Japanese history was decided: twice the armies of Kublai Khan tried to land here, on the island tip closest to Korea. Both times they were thwarted by a deadly typhoon which came to the assistance of Japan's defenders and devastated the enemy fleet. Severe storms are still quite common in Fukuoka today, but strict building regulations ensure that Pelli's Seahawk is designed to withstand both strong winds and earthquakes.

The hotel complex is situated next to a baseball stadium which can hold 40,000 spectators. Together they form a landmark from the open sea of Hakata Bay.

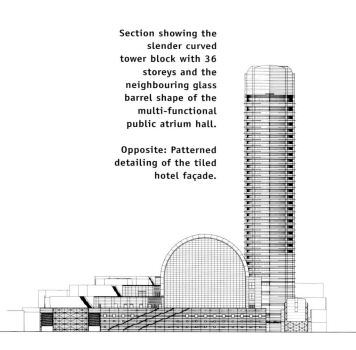

Section showing the slender curved tower block with 36 storeys and the neighbouring glass barrel shape of the multi-functional public atrium hall.

Opposite: Patterned detailing of the tiled hotel façade.

Opposite: The glass atrium houses restaurants, bars, a shopping centre and health club for the use of both the hotel guests and the general public alike. It is occupied by lush vegetation and water features, creating an indoor botanical garden.

Right: The main public areas of the hotel, including the corridors, form prestigious and calm spaces.

Below: The main floor plan; and (bottom) the roof plan.

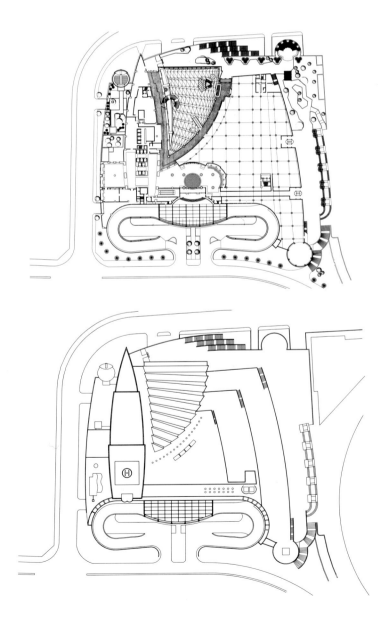

Hotel Ocean 45, Phoenix Resort Seagaia

Miyazaki, Japan, 1994

Architecture/Interior Design: Yoshinobu Ashihara Architect & Associates

THE kilometre-long beaches in Miyazaki on the south coast of Japan were not enough of an attraction on their own. Hence, the mega-project Phoenix Resort Seagaia was designed to provide everything: the ultimate beach experience, free from the vagaries of wind and weather, and a progressive complex for the national and international conference business. The centrepiece of the huge site, built on a wooded stretch of coastline, is the 154-metre-high tower of Hotel Ocean 45. The figure refers to the total number of storeys: two under the ground, 43 above it. On a triangular ground plan, and with a total floor area of 11,560 square metres, the hotel has 753 rooms with views over the sea, an atrium which is 11 storeys high, seven restaurants and the same number of bars, as well as the inevitable health club.

Arguably, this last feature is hardly necessary with Seagaia Ocean Dome, the world's largest artificial water park, just next door. A computer-controlled sliding roof, 300 metres long and 100 metres wide, opens and closes according to temperature and sunshine. When the roof is closed, this simulated south-sea paradise offers a multimedia spectacle unlike any other in Japan or elsewhere. At the press of a button huge breakers thunder in, fanfares ring out, cliffs are bathed in the pink light of an artificial sunset, magical surfers ride along the crests of the waves. This fantasy water landscape is designed to cater for more than 10,000 paying visitors each day. An arched corridor links Ocean Dome with the hotel shops and restaurants and the conference centre.

For architect Yoshinobu Ashihara, who was responsible for the overall design of Phoenix Resort Seagaia, the huge project is a role model for urban-oriented architecture: 'One can design a single, internally complete building or groups of structures in compounds for urban or regional development. But rather than simply extending the principles of the former to the design of the latter, it is in fact far more effective to take an additive approach with the parts linked by a "hidden order". Thus, the urban corridor. The linking factor is a kind of common gene manifested in formalism and functions. Outlines of a future organic, holistic order of "street aesthetics" are already emerging'. Ashihara, who spent his apprentice years in Marcel Breuer's New York studio, belongs to the old guard of Japanese modernism. He designed the Japanese pavilion for the world exhibition in Montreal in 1967. There is a certain irony in the fact that the dreams of rationally structured, park-like urban projects are seeing a late fruition in multi-million leisure complexes. However, the wonderworld of Phoenix Resort Seagaia has not proved to be the godsend Miyazaki had hoped for. Quite the reverse: the resort is operating at a loss, having accumulated a deficit of some $100 million by the end of 1997.

The Phoenix Seagaia Resort consists of the giant Ocean Dome, the hotel tower and a conference complex

Left: A section of Hotel Ocean 45.

Opposite: The atrium lobby with lounges and access to restaurant facilities.

The interior of the guest suites and
lounges is a mix of international
mainstream and Japanese
influences fitting the target groups
of high class business travellers
and tourists.

An opulently furnished double
bedroom overlooking the Miyazaki
beach.

New York, New York Hotel & Casino

Las Vegas, USA, 1997

Architecture: Gaskin & Bezanski Architecture and Engineering

Interior Design: Yates Silverman Inc.

LAS VEGAS, once America's capital of kitsch and vice, has become the nation's tourist boom town of the 1990s. The city is now ruled not by mob godfathers but by highly profitable entertainment groups who are investing in family entertainment for the masses and building ever more gigantic fantasy complexes. Las Vegas's parade of hybrid hotel-and-casino palaces is a catalogue of superlatives, and New York, New York proved itself a worthy new addition by breaking several records when it opened in early 1997. With its 155-metre-high replica of the Empire State Building and a skyline crammed with Manhattan motifs, this is the tallest building yet in the city of glitz. The complex presents a profusion of Big Apple quotations (on a 1:3 scale), approached over a 100-metre-long mini version of the Brooklyn Bridge. Curving around the skyscrapers is the high-speed rollercoaster Manhattan Express with its daredevil loops and curves.

This megalomaniac project, covering 133,200 square metres of useable floor space at a cost of more than $460 million was funded in a joint venture by MGM Grand and Primadonna Resorts. Las Vegas-based architects Gaskin & Bezanski were commissioned to design the building, while the interior decoration was designed by Californian team Yates-Silverman, who had previously fitted out the kitsch castle Excalibur and the Luxor glass pyramid for competitors. The client's project design director Joyce E. Orias summarizes the brief: 'The New York, New York Hotel & Casino was a challenge in incorporating endless popular icons from the nation's largest and most sophisticated city into a 20-acre block of real estate. Due to lack of space,

great detail was placed in theming, propping and signage of building façades. Driven by a desire to satisfy an increasingly demanding and media-savvy public, careful attention was paid in areas closest to the customer'.

In this over-the-top setting the casino features backdrops from Wall Street to Central Park, while the lobby of the 1000-seat theatre is made into a tiled subway station. Even the quieter areas are not spared: all the lavatories are decked out in NYC motifs, be it Penn Street Station, a baseball stadium, or a jazz club.

New York, New York, with its 2,035 rooms, is positioned in the upper-middle segment of the new generation of hyper hotels. By the end of the century Las Vegas's total hotel capacity is set to rise from the present 100,000 rooms to more than 160,000. Paris Casino Resort, currently under construction, will soon have more than 3,000 rooms and its Eiffel Tower replica will bring even New York New York's record into serious danger.

Opposite: The main façade of congested skyscrapers with a replica of the Statue of Liberty and the breath-taking rollercoaster 'The Manhattan Express'.

Below: Elevation showing the tight grouping of Manhattan landmarks, all built on a 1:3 scale.

Right: The reception is a glorious art déco representation of the New York underground of the 1920s and 1930s. The mahogany and burlwood front desk has a scaled down subway train circulating to entertain the guests while they are waiting to check in.

Below: The casinos are overlooked both by direct Big Apple quotes such as the perfect replica of the Stock Exchange, as well as by playful yet unmistakable American iconography.

Hard Rock Hotel & Casino

Las Vegas, USA, 1995

Architecture: Franklin D. Israel Design Associates

Interior Design Consultant: Warwick Stone

MTV made a special, live broadcast for the opening of this project, to celebrate the move into the hotel and casino business by the highly successful, international chain of Hard Rock Cafés, theme restaurants crammed with pop memorabilia. For the booming entertainment metropolis of Las Vegas, which has nine of the ten largest hotels in the US along its Strip, the new addition was a pint-sized project, costing just $102 million, with 340 rooms on 11 floors. And yet the success of the Hard Rock Hotel & Casino could be very important for the future: up to now this desert city has made its profits mainly from its popularity with older tourists. In the words of writer Mario Puzo, Las Vegas is a unique manifestation of 'the dazzling alchemy of American democratic capitalism': the Hard Rock Café with its famous recycling of rock myths and paraphernalia makes a worthy addition to the city's spectrum of kitsch and seeks to attract a younger group of customers for whom spouting volcanoes, sinking pirate ships and white tigers hold little appeal.

Peter Morton, inventor and president of the Hard Rock empire, has a clear mission: 'Our target audience is a 30-year-old yuppie who drives a BMW convertible and goes to Bruce Springsteen shows. We wanted it to be anti-Vegas, a resort to appeal to a new generation of customers'. Directly next to the Hard Rock Café,

established here for some years, he commissioned top Californian architect Franklin D. Israel to design an understated white building reminiscent of the Fifties hotel architecture of Miami Beach, its semicircular construction surrounding the extensive pool area of the Beach Club. The only landmark feature is the nearly 30-metre-high guitar-shaped sculpture over the entrance pavilion.

Inside, Hard Rock design chief Warwick Stone was responsible for the $2-million interior fittings, with rock memorabilia from Elvis to Madonna, in the typical Hard Rock mode. Alongside clothes and instruments there are showpieces like Elton John's glass-studded grand piano and the rear section of the plane in which Otis Redding crashed in 1967. The authentic paraphernalia are complemented by ubiquitous musical references: lines from songs on the walls, piano-shaped roulette tables in the casino, and chandeliers made of gilded saxophones. Even the gaming chips are decorated with song titles and portraits of stars: the $5 chip features the Red Hot Chilli Peppers' 'Give it away', the $100 chip has Tom Petty's 'You got lucky'. Guests can see live performances in 'The Joint', a concert hall with 1,400 seats. And there is canned music everywhere, even underwater in the swimming pool. The room designs, by Aero Studios of New York, transcend the tastelessness which is the norm in Las Vegas, and you can even open the windows.

The Hard Rock corporate philosophy even includes a dash of ecological awareness: 'Save the planet' is the company slogan, and politically correct illuminated signs inform guests about the disappearance of the rainforests and the steady growth in the world's population. Anyone who wants to lose with a clear conscience can play on games machines whose profits go directly to environmental organizations.

Left: A 30-metre-high model of the Fender Strato-caster guitar projects out of the reception pavilion of the Hard Rock Hotel.

Right: The casino area with a 'save the planet' chandelier.

Left: The public spaces feature a $150 million collection of rock memorabilia. The chandelier is constructed out of gold-dipped saxophones.

Right: The counter of the retail outlet situated next to the casino is inevitably in the shape of a guitar.

Left: The landscaped Beach Club offers rest from the never ending buzz of slot machines.

Sunway Lagoon Resort Hotel

Petaling Jaya, Malaysia, 1997

Architecture: Akitek Akiprima

Interior Design: Sunway Design

SUNWAY LAGOON, Malaysia's biggest theme park, was built in an abandoned mining landscape, once occupied by tin mines and granite quarries. The location for this gaudy mix of funfair and jungle adventure-park could hardly be better: between the capital Kuala Lumpur and the industrial centre of Shah Alam, only minutes away from the Sultan Aziz Shah international airport in Subang. This mega-project continues to expand at an exponential rate, matching the booming economic power of the country as a whole. The five-star luxury hotel Sunway Lagoon Resort and the Sunway Lagoon Pyramid (a conference, exhibition, shopping and leisure complex) were opened in quick succession in 1997. The driving force behind them is Malaysian tycoon Jeffrey Cheah, whose Sungei Way Group develops and operates shopping centres, commercial property and hotels not only in Malaysia but also in Cambodia, Vietnam and China. The new Sunway Lagoon ensemble is the centrepiece of this rapidly expanding empire: a fantasy town in the Arabian Nights mode, designed in a loosely-interpreted Moorish style.

The hotel section has 439 rooms on 19 storeys, including 10 honeymoon suites in prettified Art Déco and 36 themed rooms (Wild West, harem or Malaysian folklore décors). On top of this there are Japanese, Cantonese and Italo-American restaurants, as well as the

largest ballroom in the land (2,340 square metres). A new wing, to be completed in 1998, will increase the hotel's capacity by another 400 rooms. The hotel merges seamlessly with the fantasy world of the Sunway Lagoon Pyramid, named after its crude copy of the Louvre glass pyramid with a massive Sphinx portal in front of it. Conference facilities and meeting rooms are housed together in a glazed tower. Below this is a huge range of entertainments and distractions: shops, pubs in alleyways with evocative names like Cleopatra's Walk, the cyber adventures of Sega City, a ten-screen multiplex cinema, the Pyramid Ice ice rink (designed as a Swiss winter garden), and a bowling centre with 48 alleys. The superlatives continue outside the building: alongside the pool area with waterfall, Sunway Lagoon has what is supposedly the tallest wave machine in the world, on a 170-metre-long sandy beach.

Through this kingdom of kitsch winds a monorail train, which even branches off to provide a direct connection with the local rail network. The entire design of Sunway Lagoon Resort Hotel and Sunway Lagoon Pyramid was in the hands of local architects: Akitek Akiprima was responsible for the oriental fantasy architecture, while the in-house team Sunway Design designed the interior settings, which are so breathtakingly naïve that they are almost quite likeable.

Above: The main hotel entrance with a fountain of bronze deers fleeing from the hungry jaws of a tiger.

Left: The lush pool area with waterfalls in the inner courtyard of the resort complex.

Left, top: The lobby has wall murals of animals and jungle flora as well as full size silver palm trees and Egyptian style columns.

Left: The variety of themed guest rooms includes the Wild West suite with horse-wagon bed.

Right: The hotel (to the left) is only part of the huge Sunway Lagoon complex. The pyramid houses a conference centre and acts as main entrance for giant shopping and leisure facilities.

The Palace of the Lost City

Sun City, South Africa, 1992

Architecture: Wimberly Allison Tong & Goo

Interior Design: Wilson & Associates

Landscape Architecture: Patrick Watson/Top-Turf & Assoc.

HOW to turn a long-dead volcano into a gold mine: this was the feat pulled off by entertainment magnate Sol Kerzner in South Africa's Highveld. Kerzner created the hotel and casino complex Sun City on a 25-hectare plot of bush country in the former homeland of Boputhatswana. As his miniature Las Vegas grew and prospered, Kerzner decided that it needed something extra to give it an international reputation and pull in customers beyond the mainly white weekend visitors from Johannesburg and other parts of South Africa. He engaged the experienced resort architects Wimberly Allison Tong & Goo, invested more than $300 million and created, together with project architect Gerald Allison, the 'Lost City', a kingdom from the past: 'The charge from the client was this: design a luxury hotel of unprecedented opulence and originality that will lure the most sophisticated traveller. We had the odd challenge to recreate an architecture that never existed' (Allison).

This was not the end of it. The exclusive Palace of the Lost City was not going to dissociate itself from its more down-market neighbour, the resort of Sun City: hence, downhill from the hotel the architects created a huge fantasy-landscape with ruins, canyons and endless water chutes. The Bridge of Time, flanked by stone elephants, connects the fantasy area with the gambling-machine paradise of the Entertainment Center: every hour the bridge quakes dramatically, emitting steam and rumbling noises. These supposed relics of a vanished African civilization are recreated through uniquely lavish special-effect architecture.

The Palace area itself includes majestic pools, streams and ponds, mini-jungles, and a golf club nestling under huge artificial cliffs. The hotel is up to eight storeys high, with numerous towers and a floor space of 62,500 square metres. In addition to 328 rooms and 21 suites it offers the Crystal Court and Villa del Palazzo restaurants, the Tusk Bar, and a handful of shops. The whole magnificent lion-yellow creation, studded with traditional African decorations, was built in record time (only 32 months), using prefabricated concrete sections which had been treated with a special ageing process so that they looked the part. The interior design by American team Wilson & Associates is a lavish confection in the spirit of the fictional brief. The result is a dizzying but impressively crafted foray through all the clichés and legends you can think of connected with the Black Continent.

The isolated location, more than two hours' drive and nearly an hour's flight from Johannesburg, makes the impact of the Lost City all the more surreal. This themed oasis borders the Pilanesberg national park, one of the largest nature reserves in the country. Real elephants and leopards are just a few minutes away from the bronze creatures designed by South African artist Dani de Jager. The mythical setting has become a popular backdrop for international film production teams. One Australian crew even came here to make a TV series about Tarzan. The filming conditions are perfect: dense, tangled vegetation and rickety bridges over storming rapids – all in a carefully-nurtured jungle setting, and with convenient power plugs hidden in the greenery.

Left: The Palace of the Lost City is situated in a fantasy landscape of rocks, ruins, cascades and carefully planted vegetation.

Opposite: The richly frescoed cupola of the reception hall.

**Above left: The Tusk Lounge
and Bar is decorated with
African artefacts and brightly
coloured cushions from local
artisans.**

**Above: The Villa del Palazzo
Restaurant for formal dining
with a Scagliola mosaic
floor and elaborately carved
chairs with animal motifs.**

Above: The Crystal Court
restaurant is dominated by
a huge fountain with four
bronze elephants below a
bronze and crystal chandelier.
The surrounding columns
represent bamboo bundles,
topped with palm fronds
and set on elephant's feet.

The King's suite continues the African sub-continent theme with specially designed Leopard-print bedding.

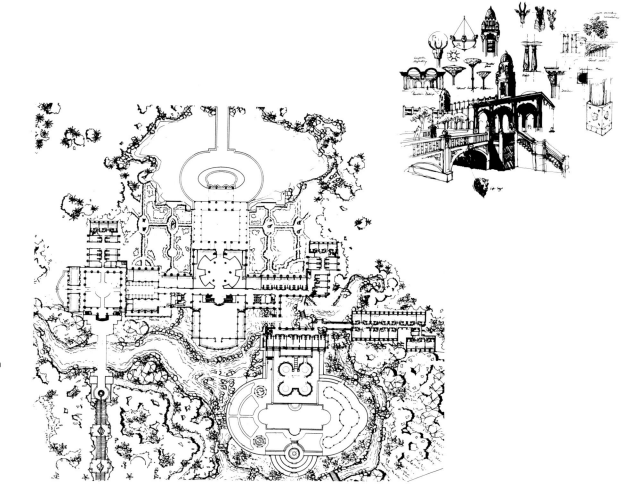

Left: The golf club house uses both artificial rock formations and prehistoric architectural forms and quotes directly from the mysterious Zimbabwe towers.

Right: Site plan and concept drawing of the open-air domes of the towers which dominate the hotel's design.

Disney's Wilderness Lodge

Lake Buena Vista, USA, 1994

Architecture: Urban Design Group

Interior Design: Wilson & Associates

THE Rocky Mountains would seem to be the perfect setting for the world's largest log cabin. In fact it stands in the flat, sultry terrain of Florida, separated only by a lake from the Magic Kingdom. Disney's Wilderness Lodge, which opened in 1994, is a unique, exotic creation among the group of theme hotels at the Walt Disney World. In place of the usual theme resorts this seven-storey building made of huge wooden tree trunks from Oregon and Montana transplants something of the elemental power of the Wild West into the otherwise rather soft-edged vacation paradise. The site cost $75 million and has 728 rooms on 55,000 square metres of useable floor space: a medium-sized project by local standards. However, unlike most other recent hotels Disney's Wilderness Lodge represents the evolution of the Disney philosophy from child-friendly architecture to authentic architectural simulation.

This process began with the appointment of the Urban Design Group from Denver, Colorado, which is rooted in the architectural traditions of American west;

it continued with the stylistic analysis of traditional lodges in US National Parks and culminated in the careful adaptation of historic models, right down to details of materials and decoration. 'To work in historic traditions of forms and materials while using modern technology and ideas to challenge and enrich those traditions. Drawing on the craftsman traditions of the west. A Rocky Mountain experience, memorable and dramatic. Similar materials used indoor and out, rock, wood. The outside combines the drama of the natural setting and protection from it. The inside contains the opposite of the outside, the geometric, formal in contrast to the organic, sensual' (Peter Dominick, Urban Design Group). Everything is artificial: the rock formations with waterfall and half-hourly geyser are imitations just as much as the building itself.

The centrepiece is the monumental six-storey atrium with a huge open fireplace in the Grand Canyon style and oversized totem poles. In all probability the huge log cabin is built using a conventional reinforced concrete structure, but at least this journey into another time does not work with cheap substitutes and vulgar imitations, at least it attempts a genuine reinterpretation of historic myths and architectural traditions.

Early American modernism defined itself in the spirit of the Arts and Crafts movement; after the turn of the century the large lodges in picturesque mountain settings or nature reserves provided majestic evidence of an independent style, a tradition which influenced later architects like Frank Lloyd Wright. The aim of connecting with this tradition and transplanting a reincarnation of this cultural heritage into the Disney fantasy world is a brilliant success. Interior designers Wilson & Associates made a decisive contribution in this respect, developing a special iconography from Indian motifs and other quotations from the Wild West. If some figures from the Disney kingdom creep in too, subversively, then this is both legitimate and enjoyable: after all, the comical chipmunks Chip N' Dale are featured on the Wilderness Lodge graphics.

Waterfalls, an artificial geyser and dramatic rock formations form the stage set for the biggest log cabin in the world.

Opposite: The impressive atrium lobby is surrounded by the open guest floors. The canyon styled chimney of the giant fireplace rises through the ceiling.

Above: The guest rooms with
contemporary comfort don't overstress
the Western iconography.

Above right: Lobby with glazed front
to the landscaped water garden.

Disney's BoardWalk, Walt Disney World

Lake Buena Vista, USA, 1996

Architecture: Robert A.M. Stern Architects

Interior Design: Design One/Robert A.M. Stern

'BUILDING a Dream': this was the title of an exhibition on the history of Disney architecture which was shown in the United States pavilion at the Architecture Biennale in Venice in 1996. No-one has pursued the American dream more intensively than New York architect Robert A. M. Stern, who has worked for the entertainment group for the last ten years. He now sits on the Disney board as an advisor, having designed corporate buildings like the Casting Center in Orlando and the Feature Animation Building in Burbank, as well as five large hotel complexes for Walt Disney World Resort in Florida and Disneyland Paris Resort – not forgetting the holiday home of company chief Michael Eisner in Aspen, Colorado.

Stern's latest project, Disney's BoardWalk recreates an idealized holiday scene from the turn of the century. It is set on a 4.5-hectare plot, alongside an artificial lagoon, and presents a perfect self-contained world of small-scale buildings, its streets and squares lined with old-fashioned street lights. The project cost a total of $83 million and covers an area of more than 100,000 square metres. It includes a hotel with 378 beds and the Disney Vacation Club with 528 suites, a conference centre and a multitude of restaurants and shops. Stern describes his models as follows: 'The hotel takes its architectural cue from rambling colonial revival-style hotels of New England. Where the vacation club faces a canal, the building is reflecting an early twentieth-

century American tradition that combined classicism with vernacular cottage architecture to create the Bungalow Style. Recalling a country fair that might have existed next to a resort town, the pool is a private but lively gathering spot for the resort. The meeting facility is a sprawling bracketed Victorian-Gothic inspired hall such as might have served as the community social and cultural center of a seaside town one hundred years ago'.

The focal point of this nostalgic compendium is a miniaturized Main Street, the king pin of all Mickey Mouse architecture: this is the classical starting point of all Disney Theme parks from Anaheim and Orlando to Paris and Tokyo. Disney's BoardWalk expands the pastel-coloured, theatrical world to include functional buildings: these are intended not just as stopovers for visitors to the Magic Kingdom, Epcot and Disney-MGM Studios, but also as an attractive backdrop for longer holidays. Disney's BoardWalk vacation club offers a wealth of activities and courses, taking it a stage further down the route from the entertainment-attraction to the real-life simulation of idealized living environments.

A few kilometres away Stern is designing and building his first complete town, in collaboration with other retro-colleagues: this pretty, interpretation of a historical settlement is called Celebration. Its lucky inhabitants will be able to enjoy the Disney experience, that archetypal celebration of the American dream, every day of their lives.

The BoardWalk's *porte cochere* is the gate to a revival of an American holiday dreamworld.

Stern's design is intended to create
the atmosphere of a turn-of-the-
century resort town. The buildings
are a mixture of classical references
and the colonial style of the white
board houses of New England.

The Atlantic Dance Hall, a 1930s high-style, Art-Deco-inspired, big-band night club which anchors the north end of Disney's Boardwalk.

Carpeting detail in the conference centre. The retro-minded interior design was also in the hands of architect Robert M. Stern.

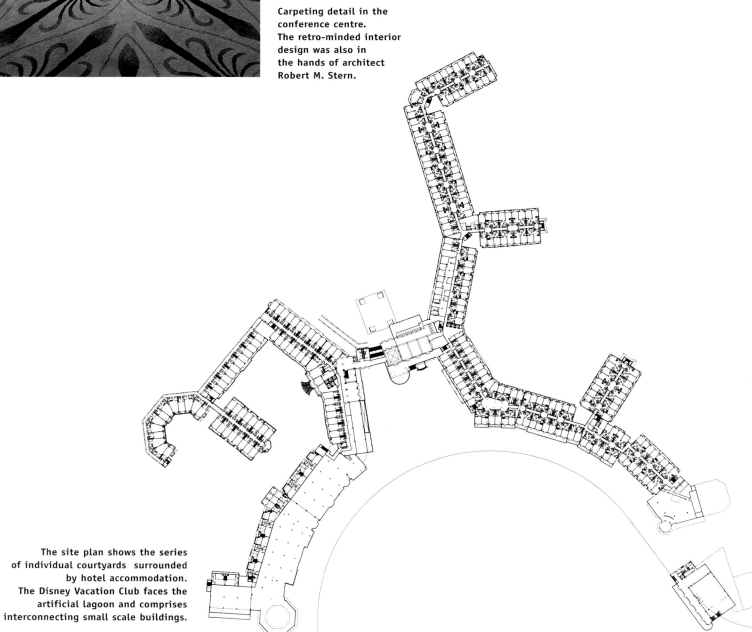

The site plan shows the series of individual courtyards surrounded by hotel accommodation. The Disney Vacation Club faces the artificial lagoon and comprises interconnecting small scale buildings.

Shutters on the Beach

Santa Monica, USA, 1993

Architecture: Hill Glazier Architects

Interior Design: Intradesign/Paul Draper & Associates

THIS project was intended to be something quite out of the ordinary: its starting point was the idea of a beach hotel in the city, while its form looks back to the Shingle Style of traditional Southern Californian beach architecture. The three-part ensemble with its dazzling white balconies and light grey wooden façades radiates a seaside mood even though it is only a few minutes away from the hectic metropolis of Los Angeles. The architects, Hill Glazier, summarized their design principles as follows: 'Because the client asked that we design the building to look as though it had always been there, our inspiration became the turn-of-the-century beach bungalows which were once found along the Santa Monica and Malibu coast. To achieve the intimate scale the hotel was designed to appear as three small buildings rather than one large massing'.

The triple division of the site, which has some 16,150 square metres of usable floor space, is matched by its functional divisions. The two-storey Beach House nearest to the sea houses the café-bistro Pedals and the restaurant One Pico. Next comes the four-storey Boat House, joined to Beach House by the lobby and the bar, followed by the six-storey, horseshoe-shaped Ocean House. Boat House and Ocean House, which stand on either side of the large pool terrace, have a total of 198 rooms and suites. The architecture revels in motifs from the past – with window blinds, beamed ceilings and open fireplaces – without the slightest hint of nostalgic stuffiness. The rooms are light, comfortable and inviting with their blue and white upholstery, luxurious bedding and, of course, the white shutters that give the hotel its name. An unusual feature is the internal window between the bathroom and the bedroom: this transforms the oval whirlpool bath, giving it a grandstand view over the sea. The hotel also offers an excellently equipped health club and the ballroom, The Grand Salon, which can accommodate more than 200 people.

This traditional five-star luxury has not, however, entirely erased all traces of the colourful local beach culture: guests can hire bicycles and rollerblades free of charge, and the eccentric spot of Venice is not far off. The designers came up with a stunning solution for one of the drawbacks of the location, a public access road running from one end of the hotel site to the other: they placed the swimming pool and the sundeck on a bridge construction over the road; underneath it they created a practical delivery area with access to the underground car park.

Left: The hotel buildings employ a turn-of-the-century Californian seaside style. The Beach House shown here is heading towards the ocean.

Opposite: The bedrooms with whitewashed panelled walls, club chairs and overstuffed beds offer a cosy informality. Each one has shuttered balconies which give the hotel its name.

Left: The brightly coloured pool area sits amidst white boarded verandas. It has been cleverly positioned on the second floor above a main service road which runs through the hotel site.

Opposite: Pedals café is situated in the boathouse overlooking the sea. It has a tiled floor and open-air kitchen and is intended for informal eating.

Below: The pool level floor plan shows the hotel's three main structures: the square beach house joined to the boat house by the lobby behind which is the ocean block containing most of the guest rooms.

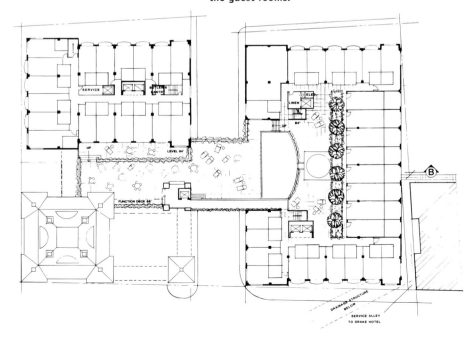

Pousada Santa Maria de Flor da Rosa

Crato, Portugal, 1995

Architecture/Interior Design: Joao Luís Carrillho da Graça

'ITS unusual setting in the open plain, the hybridity of its warlike, monastic and palatial character, its mediterranean cloister and septentrional tower build the enigma. The collision of fragments of such different periods is unified by granite. What we now find seems rather perfect, though. Perfect as a contemplation and visiting site. The repairs progress. Archaeology teaches us how to look at stones. The project's aim is to intensify the possibility of visiting the existing building, privatizing and occupying it as little as possible, rereading it and opening it to new interpretations.' This is how Lisbon architect Joao Luís Carrillho da Graça describes the extremely tricky task of turning a national monument into a five-star hotel.

The monastery fortress of Flor da Rosa is located near the town of Crato in the Alto Alentejo to the west of Lisbon; it was built by Alvaro Gonçales Pereira in 1356. It was his son Nuno Alvares Pereira who vanquished the Spanish invaders from Castile in the famous battle of Aljubarotto in 1385, thus finally securing Portugal's independence. However, this famous past was not enough to sustain the mighty fortress, once used by knights of the Maltese order. For many years the monastery and the church stood empty, and more than fifty years ago a fire devastated the historic site, leaving it in ruins. Recently Portugal's national institute for historic monuments attempted to conserve what could be saved, but the resources available were not sufficient for the job.

The idea of converting Santa Maria Flor da Rosa into a hotel, as part of the prestigious Pousada chain, might have been a disaster, as Portugal has no proper building protection legislation. It was all the more fortunate that the architect laid the emphasis on preserving and restoring, opening and separating. The church, the cloister and other parts of the monastery site remain open to visitors and a museum has been set up. With great care the architect converted some of the less prominent areas into a lobby, restaurant, bar and suites. Most of the rooms (24 in total) are accommodated in a new wing, which provides a sharp contrast to the historical building with its radical angularity. The swimming pool and the orange grove which was planted to form a new inner courtyard are not visible until you enter the reception. The principle followed throughout, both inside and outside, is additive rather than reductive. The internal furnishings, some designed by the architect, are mostly modern, but they do not overshadow the architectural heritage: indeed, the contrast serves to highlight the uniqueness of the historical setting. This ensures that the hotel is not a showy usurper, pushing itself into the foreground, and the dignity of the historical site is preserved.

Right: Most of the hotel is situated in a new wing while less historically important parts of the old monastery fortress have been turned into a lobby, bar, restaurant and suites. The majority of the historic landmark is a museum open to the general public.

Opposite: Lounge seating adjoining the restaurant. The architects saved the original fabric wherever possible, adding understated modern furnishings to bring luxury to the four star Pousada without destroying the historical ambience.

Above: The contemporary part of
the hotel is in a modern angular
and minimalist style in contrast to
the ancient architecture. The
pool is only visible once inside the
reception area.

Right: Ground floor plan, showing
both the old and new structures.

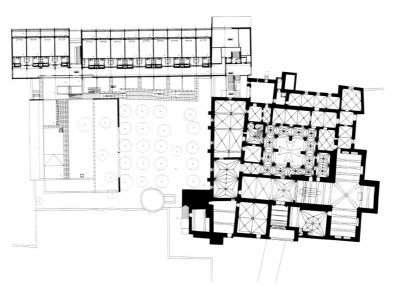

Above: The interior of the Don Alvaro Suite

The Regent Resort Chiang Mai

Chiang Mai, Thailand, 1995

Architecture: Chulathat Kitibutr, Chiangmai Collaborative Architects

CHIANG Mai, in north Thailand, was once a favourite destination for international backpackers; now it has been discovered for luxury tourism, and investment and visitors are pouring into the city. The Regent Resort, which opened in 1995, shows that costly construction projects in the five-star category can have truly beneficial effects. The eight-hectare hotel site is ten kilometres from the city centre, nestling in the lush vegetation of the Mae Rim valley amidst rice terraces, wooded hills and streams; it is a perfect example of architecture designed to suit its surrounding landscape.

The design commission was given to a local team, and project-leading architect Chulathat Kitibutr's priority was to integrate the hotel with the culture of the region: 'The design concept comes from that of a traditional northern Thai Village, it is modelled on the style used in the foothills, where there are plenty of paddy fields. The basic layout resembles that of traditional Lanna residences'. The historic kingdom of Lanna – the name means 'land of a million paddy fields' – came into being in 1296, and its cultural heritage lives on all around Chiang Mai today.

The Regent Resort project was designed to draw extensively on this heritage. The high, open entrance is reminiscent of old village temples; around this central point on the gently sloping terrain are 16 two-storey houses, each containing four guest apartments, arranged in a horseshoe pattern. Below the lobby building are two terraces with restaurants, shops, a bar and the pool. Ten more condominium villas with a total of 24 luxury residences and a tennis and health club complete the hotel complex. As for the landscaping, there was no need to create an idyllic setting here: it was just a question of letting nature take its course. There is even a small herd of water buffalo, which shares the grassy areas of the complex with the paying guests.

The interior designers, Abacus Design, borrowed motifs and materials from the rich Lanna heritage in their designs for the entrance pavilion, restaurants and rooms. Local textiles and crafts have a prominent place, while the floor coverings are a mixture of teak, sandstone and local Mae Rim tiles. Even the uniforms worn by the hotel staff, designed by Thailand's leading fashion designer Nagara, continue the Lanna theme. This meticulous deference to local traditions has a dual function. On the one hand it signals a new, thoughtful type of tourism that respects the country's natural and cultural riches. On the other, it also forms part of a project initiated by the king of Thailand to unlock the region's economic potential and entice mountain farmers away from the illegal but highly profitable opium trade.

Right: View across the resort, embedded in its own paddy fields. The architecture is in the style of the traditional Lanna culture of the region.

Opposite: Bathroom window overlooking a secluded courtyard. The carved wings or 'galae' at the tips of pitched roofs and wall niches are typical of the architecture in the villages of the northern foothills.

Kingfisher Bay Resort and Village

Fraser Island, Australia, 1992

Architecture/Interior Design: Guymer Bailey Architects

QUEENSLAND, with its wealth of sun and beaches, attracts more tourists than any other state in Australia. The Gold Coast near Brisbane is the busiest and most popular holiday destination on the entire continent. However, times are changing and the straightforward beach holiday of the past is giving way to more sophisticated holiday concepts. Right at the top of the list, as far as the travel industry is concerned, is eco-friendly tourism, officially defined as 'nature-based tourism that includes an educational component and is managed to be sustainable'.

The state-owned company Queensland Tourism Industry has created a model eco-friendly holiday paradise on Fraser Island: the Kingfisher Bay Resort and Village. Fraser Island is the world's largest sand island, a natural paradise some 120 kilometres in length, with 40 natural freshwater lakes, large stretches of rainforest, marshes and countless sandy beaches. There are whales in the bays and herds of dingos in the bush. UNESCO has listed the island as a protected natural site and the new hotel complex, built on a 65-hectare plot, initially met with strong resistance from conservationists. Yet despite its size the project is in every respect a model of thoughtful, minimally invasive tourism. A case study by the UNEP (United Nations Environment Programme Industry and Environment) came to the following conclusion: 'Kingfisher Bay was built to strict environmental guidelines with the aim of offering a modern resort to blend harmoniously with the island's sensitive eco-system'.

The architecture, by Brisbane-based team Guymer Bailey, incorporates features of the local architectural tradition and its low-level buildings (no more than two storeys at most) nestle below the treetops. The central pavilion, covered in corrugated iron, houses the reception, restaurants, shops and conference rooms; fanning out around it are the guest wings with 152 rooms. In addition there are more than 100 single bungalows dotted around in the surrounding landscape: most of these are privately owned. The latest phase of the project saw the completion of Wilderness Lodge, with 144 beds, offering a low-price alternative to the existing four-star facilities.

The project's exemplary value, however, derives not so much from its architecture (although this is certainly remarkable), but from its less visible qualities. Because of the unstable, marshy ground on which the site was built, the foundations had to be laid on wooden piles driven 20 metres down into the ground. In order to restore the plant life that had been disrupted during this work, native plant varieties were cultivated in a special nursery. For landscaping purposes, the builders used earth from excavations on the site, as far as possible; where imported soil was used this was taken only from pollution-free sources. All the dredgers and bulldozers were sterilized before use. The drinking water comes from springs on the island itself, while waste water is treated using a three-stage biogenetic purification process. Refuse generated on site is shipped off to the nearest mainland port.

The programme of activities for guests also reflects the awareness that natural sites are a vital resource for the tourist industry, too, and must be preserved intact. One of the hotel directors is responsible for environmental matters, and there are ten full-time rangers who run wildlife safari bush walks and whale observation tours. Of course, guests can choose to spend their time lazing about by the pool: and if Kingfisher Bay's four swimming pools are not enough for them, Fraser Island has an ample supply of deserted beaches.

Left: The main building of the resort is kept at low level using amorphous shapes to blend into the unspoilt nature reserve of Fraser Island.

Opposite: The airy lobby is situated below a glass and corrugated iron structure supported by narrow piles.

Pool deck in front of the reception
area and restaurant building.

Right: Interior of the budget accommodation Wilderness Lodge, the newest addition to the resort's guest facilities.

Below right: Site plan.

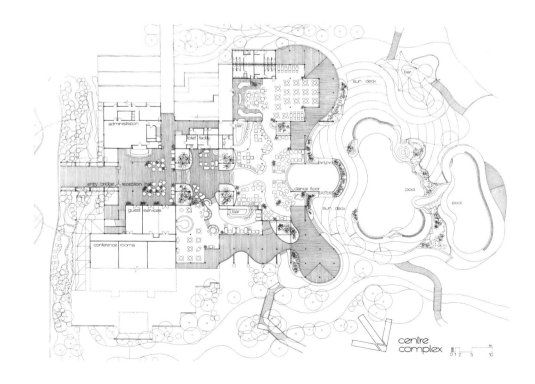

Makalili Private Game Reserve

Transvaal, South Africa, 1996

Architecture and Interior Design: Silvio Rech

THE South African founders of the Conservation Corporation founded their fast-growing business on three principles: protecting the environment, promoting the local economy through eco-tourism, and making a profit at the same time. The company now operates over twenty Game Lodges, in the top segment of the market, in South Africa, Namibia, Kenya and Zanzibar. Investors include the Getty clan, the Japanese Sakura Bank, the British Welfare Trust, and the pension fund of a South African chemical workers' union. The corporate philosophy is very convincing. The smaller, more attractive, more isolated and more expensive the lodges in the wilderness, the better it is for both wildlife and visitors. The former remain protected from gawping masses; the latter enjoy the benefits of belonging to an exclusive clientele.

The Makalili Private Game Reserve in the province of Transvaal, some 60 kilometres from the Kruger National Park, provides an excellent example of how this model functions. The pasture land of four farms in the Lowveld of Mpumalanga, covering several tens of thousands of hectares, were systematically re-populated with warthogs, hyenas, leopards, elephants, lions and rhinos. The riverbank of the Makhutswi River was chosen as the location for the lodge, Johannesburg architect Silvio Rech was commissioned to design the site, and local craftworkers were engaged to build the project. This may sound simple, but on-site this kind of project can run into huge problems due to the lack of an efficient infrastructure and local workers' inexperience in building high-class huts for high-paying tourists. 'You have to spend a lot of time on site, of course. It's a question of synthesising influences and inventing a language. The whole idea is to allow the local artists freedom to experiment with their own skills. At the end of the day the entire design is enhanced by that creative energy. The irregular angles and rough finishes don't really abide by the laws of normal architecture, yet the result is quite sophisticated' (Silvio Rech).

Everything was produced by hand, from the specially fired bricks to the wrought-iron partitions and the individually cast door handles. The free use of traditions and quotations resulted in a picturesque little village, with four separate sections of 12 guest units, extending along the riverbank. The architect and his motley crew of assistants did not attempt a synthetic stylistic plagiarism: with their uninhibited composition of borrowings they created a piece of Africa, which can claim authenticity in its own right. Red chimneys

Above: A thatch-roofed hut contains the main living and dining rooms. The style borrows freely from the vernacular and creates a new sort of kraal.

Opposite: The guest room is dominated by a huge mosquito net suspended from Masai-spear hangers and an open brick fireplace for chilly evenings.

rise out of the bungalow roofs like anthills; inside, Masai spears hold the mosquito nets over the enormous beds; the showers are outside in the open air.

No luxury is spared in all the Lodges of the Conservation Corporation: pools, restaurants and impeccable service are designed to make this encounter with the wilderness into a pleasurable and exciting experience. The day begins at five in the morning with a three-hour safari tour, in the afternoon there is a bush walk, before supper there is another four-hour cross-country jeep tour. Guests are never allowed to forget that there is no fence to separate them from the wild country around them. One night a tourist had a deadly encounter with a lioness on the short walk from the restaurant to the bungalow: since then, rangers armed with shotguns accompany guests after nightfall, even on the shortest journeys.

Opposite: Where possible the interior decorations have been hand-made on site and local materials used. The dining area utilises brightly coloured bold Abidjan braids and Kenyan fabrics. The room divider is made from mud-plastered earth bricks, again individually made and fired in local workshops and etched with drawings by native craftsmen.

Above: The comfort needs of wealthy globetrotters are met with sophisticated basics. The mosaic terrazzo floor in the bathroom is laid in a random ethnic design, the tub stands free against the clay plastered wall.

Right: Rooms are open on all four sides with folding shutters for extra privacy if needed. They have verandas overlooking the surrounding countryside as well as individual viewing platforms or 'salas'.

Compass Point Beach Club

Nassau, Bahamas, 1995

Architecture/Interior Design: Barbara Hulanicki

CHRIS Blackwell has occupied a unique place in the pop music scene for nearly 40 years. His record label, Island Records, founded in Jamaica in 1959, exported ska music (in the 1960s) and reggae (in the 1970s), first to England and from there to the rest of the world. As if this was not enough, his discoveries were some of the most creative bands of their day, including Traffic, Free, Jethro Tull, King Crimson and Roxy Music. His long, successful career stretches from the very first international hit, Millie's 'My Boy Lollipop', to present-day stars including U2, Melissa Etheridge, P.J. Harvey and Pulp.

Since music giant Polygram took over his record label (paying hundreds of millions of dollars for the privilege), Blackwell has revealed a real knack for his new sideline as hotel operator: his colourful Outpost chain now encompasses half a dozen Art Déco establishments in Miami Beach and a few small, elegant resorts scattered across the Caribbean. 'At Island Records, I put together very different artists under one umbrella. With Island Outpost, I am doing something similar. Each place is a theatre where a different play is performed. Each property has its own distinct character, but what they share is a common sensibility or aesthetic that makes them appealing to a certain kind of person. It's simple and basic. With each project, I'm attempting to do something very special. For this reason, I believe they will all make financial sense in the long run. In our case, we financed ourselves so it's not the same rules as in the hotel business. An insurance company or bank is sure to think you're nuts' (Blackwell).

The chain expanded to the Bahamas in 1995 with the Compass Point Beach Club, and here Blackwell was operating on very familiar territory. The cheerful hut village on the sandy beach is located right next to the legendary Compass Point Recording Studios, where classic albums like Dire Straits's 'Communiqué' and Bob Marley's 'Babylon by Bus' were recorded. Thirteen wooden huts and cottages are grouped together with a pool and landing stage, forming a colourful holiday village under palm trees. The gables are decorated with simple wood-carvings, and inside the bungalows conditions are picturesquely spartan, with bare wood, exposed-beam ceilings, simple furniture and practical fittings. A complete kitchenette is hidden behind wide folding doors.

For the design of this gaudy Caribbean paradise Blackwell turned to an old friend from the golden age of Swinging London: Barbara Hulanicki, founder of the Biba boutiques and designer of the incredible Knightsbridge store that delighted customers with its luxuriant Art Déco psychedelia that finally drove her to bankruptcy. Now she had found another project ideally suited to her talents, on the other side of the Atlantic. As well as designing Compass Point, Hulanicki was also responsible for the interior design of a few Outpost hotels in Miami Beach.

Blackwell's instinctive gamble on the synergy of music and the hotel business has clearly hit the mark. As a provider of accommodation for rockstars, great and small, and the fashionable clientele that follows in their wake, he may well succeed in following up the 'finest small record company in the world' with the greatest small hotel chain.

Left: Sun deck with jetty on the beachfront of Compass Point resort.

Opposite: Vivid colours and octagonal shaped wooden guest huts form a hip Bahamas village.

new grand hotels

The myth of the grand hotel as a temporary aristocratic residence, a palace for travellers, is seeing an unexpected renaissance in our current *fin de siècle* period. Decadently expensive, over-decorated, Americanized *nouveau-riche* palaces and opulent restorations of historic residences are not at the forefront of this trend. The most striking examples of contemporary grandeur are new projects or conversions of diverse historical monuments, from a courtesan's palace in Dresden to a dungeon fortress on the Bosporus. Their interior design develops alternatives to monotonous ostentation, refers to national and regional cultural traditions, integrates contemporary furniture design, and seeks to formulate a new luxury style influenced by the Art Déco tradition.

Park Hyatt

Tokyo, Japan, 1994

Architecture: Kenzo Tange Associates

Interior Design: John Morford

THE three glass pillars of the Shinjuku Park Tower stand in a stepped row, soaring up into the sky over Tokyo. The Park Hyatt hotel occupies the upper sections of this glittering, 52-storey ensemble. The huge complex, designed by Kenzo Tange Associates, has a total floor area of 264,140 square metres, and the 14 storeys of the hotel take up the best 33,000 of this. Express lifts catapult the guests from the entrance lobby into this unconventional house-in-the-clouds. The Sky Lobby on the 41st floor, with its adjoining Sky Lounge, lives up to its name: fully glazed walls offer dizzying views over the Japanese metropolis and across to Mount Fujijama. Through the pyramid-shaped roof structure all you can see is sun, clouds and stars. This spectacle of transparency and limitlessness culminates at the top of the other two towers of which one houses the luxury pool of the extensive fitness centre Club in the Park. The other, the highest of the trio, is the setting for the panoramic restaurant, New York Grill.

In Tokyo terms the Park Hyatt, with 178 rooms and suites, is one of the smaller-scale five-star hotels. Thus it is without irony that the American interior designer John Morford, who lives in Hong Kong, can describe his task as 'Making a small hotel which is part of an enormous building seem small and personal'. The design that looks so natural and effective was in fact the result of a tough struggle with very complex spatial conditions. Morford had to bridge large distances, horizontally and vertically, and to integrate the disparate structure of the three tower sections into an artistically satisfying and

Left: The hotel is situated on the top 15 floors of the three towers of the Shinjuku Park complex.

Below: The fully glazed Sky Lounge with its indoor bamboo garden is located under the rooftop of the lowest tower.

functional hotel design. 'The main challenge was making the process of getting to various hotel spaces understandable and pleasant since it is necessary to change elevators and to travel considerable distances between the tiers. The most important features are the progressions of spaces, beginning at the bottom of Park Tower and ending at the 52nd floor New York Grill. They make the journey entertaining' (John Morford).

Other stylistic features which the interior designer skillfully introduced in the restaurants and in the well-proportioned guest rooms are just as interesting. Here, there is none of the expensive glitz which often runs wild in luxury-class business hotels. Instead, there are large-scale works of art commissioned from the painter Valerio Adami and the photographer Vera Mercer. Materials used include many precious woods, among them 2000-year-old elm from Japan, ebony from east India, mahogany from South America and walnut from North America. However, it took more than just intelligent interior design to ensure that guests could feel entirely comfortable high above the Japanese capital. Because the most important structural task was to make the construction safe from the elements: 'As the hotel is located on the upper levels of a high rise structure, particular attention was paid to concerns about earthquakes and high wind conditions. For example the pool in the fitness club required special technical measures to prevent the water from spilling over during the building's oscillations' (Kenzo Tange).

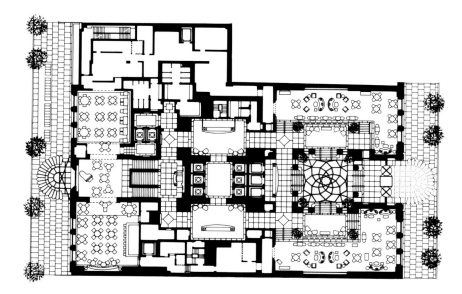

Preceding pages: The majestic staircases are the overture to the sequence of major public spaces as lounges, restaurants and ballrooms.

Left: Floor plan of the lobby level.

Left: The bar area decorated with original drawings from the 1920s by Kimon Nicolaides and a ceiling design by CSP.

Right: The guest room interiors avoid any pastiche five-star opulence and indicate instead a high standard of contemporary, exclusive comfort.

Park Hyatt

Johannesburg, South Africa, 1995

Architecture: GAPP

Interior Design: Hirsch Bedner Associates

THE city of Johannesburg is the boom town of the new South Africa and since the end of apartheid it has become a focus of international business life. The Park Hyatt that opened here in the late autumn of 1995 was the first new business hotel in the luxury category: a marker of political and economic change, signalling the opening of South Africa to the markets and companies of the world. Hirsch Bedner Associates of Atlanta, the usual choice for most Hyatt Group projects, were commissioned to design the hotel interior. Just because they were old hands did not mean that they chose the obvious mainstream solution, however: in fact they took a close look at the characteristics of their location: 'The brief was to design an urban business hotel in a contemporary, fast-paced city. The design was to be appropriate for domestic and international business people, reflecting total influences and design elements within a five-star international quality environment. The African influences are taken as inspiration for design motifs. Elements are used in a different context from the traditional use to create a feeling or impression rather than a direct interpretation' (Hirsch Bedner Associates).

The eight-storey building encompasses 250 guest rooms, a restaurant, bar, conference area, business centre and health club. The interior designers chose gold as the leading colour in honour of the region's great mining tradition. Large sections of the walls are covered with shimmering gold leaf. The red slate and black granite of the floors in the lobby and other public spaces come from Rustenburg and Transvaal, the dark woods of the panelling and furniture are from African sapele trees, the leather cladding of the pillars also comes from local sources. Instead of textile wall coverings, the guest rooms have bare plaster tinted with earth colours colours. The décor of the Restaurant-Café 191 is also less sophisticated than usual: the bare brick walls, black iron girders and waxed wooden tiles are reminiscent of industrial architecture.

The client, a South African pension fund, stipulated in conjunction with Hyatt that the contracts for individual works should be given in preference to South African firms and craftworkers. This may have complicated matters as far as deadlines were concerned, but it yielded clear benefits in terms of artistic diversity. Proof of this can be seen in the varied marquetry of the panelling and furniture and in the engaging irregularity of the warm-coloured paintwork, infinitely preferable to industrial uniformity. The Park Hyatt in Johannesburg is a glittering achievement – even without the gold leaf.

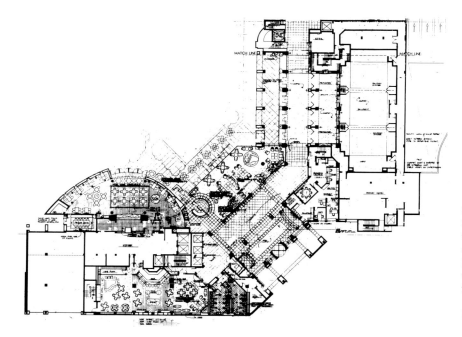

Opposite: Local materials have been used throughout the hotel as far as possible. The floor of red slate and black granite is from Rustenburg and the Transvaal, the wooden reception desk is made from the African sapele tree.

Left: Ground floor plan.

The exposed steel trusses and brick wall cladding of the restaurant relate to the industrial mining past of the Johannesburg region.

Left, above: Bathroom unit with built-in shelves and marble tiling.

Left: Natural earth tones have been used as well as natural materials to bring warmth to the guest rooms and suites. International luxury is met by African motifs and the use of selected traditional furnishing and craft techniques.

The Four Seasons Hotel

Istanbul, Turkey, 1996

Architecture: Yalçin Özüekren

Interior Design: Sinan Kafadar, Metex Design Group

AT THE Four Seasons Hotel in Istanbul a select clientele can pay handsomely for the unusual pleasure of sleeping behind prison walls. The gaol in question was built in 1917, shortly before the collapse of the Ottoman empire; its well-preserved building is located close to Hagia Sophia and the Blue Mosque. Today the only reminders of its dark days as a dungeon, when inmates included prominent political prisoners like the writer Nazim Hikmet, are the thick walls and a few of the original barred windows. Now the erstwhile penal institution has been converted into a highly distinctive top-class hotel, thanks to a budget of $25 million and a design which draws on Turkish architecture and culture.

Sinan Kafadar, project architect with the Metex Design Group of Istanbul, who were entrusted with the conversion, lists the guiding principles behind the project: 'Authentic atmosphere, local craftsmanship, interior design fitting the architecture. When designing the hotel, the main purpose was to remind the guest where he is. The style of the late Ottoman and national

designs were targeted'. The building is painted in a glowing yellow ochre, and the battlements and towers are magically illuminated at night. The former prison yard has become a palm-bordered restaurant oasis. In the interior, Turkish materials predominate: marble, mosaic tiles, wood, wrought iron. Most of the walls were painted using the traditional spatula technique. The geometrical patterns and motifs are oriental in origin.

Compared with the overblown Americanized affluence which is the hallmark of the Four Seasons group in its other locations, the Istanbul hotel makes a thoroughly distinctive contribution to luxury hotel design. Guests' expectations in terms of comfort and luxury are met to the full, without suppressing all historical-cultural authenticity. You do not have to look out of the window to remember where you are, in this unique city teeming with the relics of Byzantine and Ottoman power. All the details reflect this rich historical context: from small minarets on the bedposts and the carved furniture in the 67 guest rooms and suites, to the magnificently worked carpets in the bar and the lobby, and above all the art works on display – a mixture of antiques and many contemporary pieces.

The conversion of the prison into a world-class hotel is exemplary: all alterations to the historic fabric of the building were undertaken with the greatest of care. Many of the old room arrangements and entrances were left unchanged or were only carefully modified. On the other hand, it is entirely understandable that some of the thick cell walls had to be removed on the guest floors in order to make space for present-day five star suites, and this is of no real consequence: the new ground plans fit harmoniously into the old structure.

Left: View towards the lobby area.

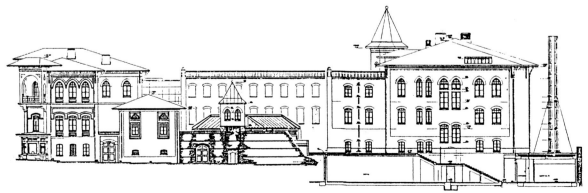

Above: The former prison yard was
turned into a palatial oasis.

Left: Elevation of the building.

Above: The guest rooms and suites
are carefully designed in individual
styles relating to late Ottoman
interiors. Some offer splendid
views of the Istanbul landmarks.

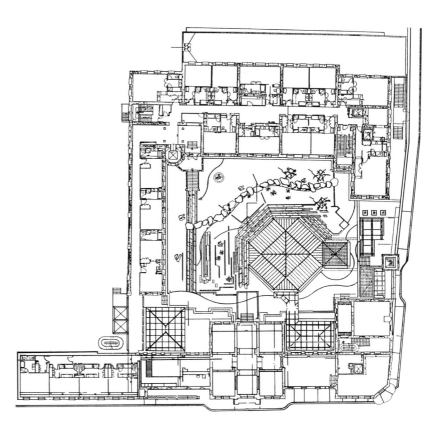

Right: Ground-floor plan.

Above: Late Ottoman styling has been used in the detailing of the bar, as seen in the geometric motifs of the rug and the specially commissioned paintings by Turkish artist Timur Kerim Incedayi.

Kempinski Hotel Taschenbergpalais

Dresden, Germany, 1995

Architecture: AIC Bauplanungs- und Consultinggesellschaft/
Planungsbüro Versammlungsstätten Dresden

Interior Design: AB 'Living Designs'

T HE night of 13 February 1945, when Allied bombing reduced Dresden's Baroque splendours to dust and rubble, it also sealed the fate of the Taschenbergpalais. This elegant small palace, close to the castle, the Zwinger, the Semperoper and Brühl's Elbe terrace, was erected by August II, known as August the Strong, Kurfürst of Saxony and King of Poland, for his mistress Anna Constantia, Countess Cosel. He appointed court architect Matthäus Daniel Pöppelmann for this very personal project, requesting the practical addition of a secret passageway between the royal residence and his mistress's apartment. However, Anna Constantia was not to enjoy her new home for long. After she had borne August three children, whom he acknowledged as his legitimate heirs, she was sent into exile in 1716. After this the Taschenbergpalais was converted and extended a number of times and used as the residence of the crown prince. After the abdication of the Wettin dynasty, Saxon bureaucrats occupied the building in the 19th century.

The inferno caused by the Allied air raid in 1945 left only burnt-out ruins. It was a miracle that these pitiful remains escaped the bland Socialist building frenzy, which affected Dresden more than anywhere else in the GDR; salvation finally came in the guise of an investor from the west after German reunification. The

99-year lease cost DM45 million, while the historic reconstruction along with extensions added another DM250 million. The result was the Kempinski Hotel Taschenbergpalais, and the best thing about this five-star hotel is that the huge sums invested in it are not the first thing that strike you.

The architect partners – AIC Bauplanungs- und Consultinggesellschaft from Munich and the Planungsbüro Versammlungsstätten Dresden – reconstructed Pöppelmann's overall composition and designed extensions which match the original building in terms of scale and structure. Inside, the main staircase was rebuilt following the original design. However, the interiors by Swedish team AB Living Designs avoid overblown pseudo-historicism: their design is a restrained, eclectic mix of classical and contemporary, of historical quotation and modern style. The commission for the interior furnishings was given to the long-established Deutsche Werkstätten Hellerau, just outside Dresden. The new hotel has a total floor space of 45,000 square metres 213 rooms (average size 48 square metres), along with the Intermezzo and Vestibule restaurants, the Allegro bar, a pool, sauna and health club under the roof, a large ballroom in the basement and a four-level underground car park. Not forgetting the obligatory Meissen china shop, of course.

Yet even today the Taschenbergpalais will not let us forget the bitterest hour in its 300-year history: Pöppelmann's central *risalto* was not painted over in the flawless pale yellow/cream colour used for the other sections of the building. The faded surface of the façade with its dark patches still bears witness to the terrible fires in which the old city of Dresden perished.

Right: The Baroque palace was rebuilt from ruins and new wings were added. The historic façade still carries the burn marks resulting from the 1945 Allied bombing.

Above: The carefully restored, original
grand staircase is one of the few
features that relate to the great past
of the Taschenbergpalais.

Above: The Crown Prince's Suite has six rooms and caters for the state guests who visit the once more noble capital of post-communist Saxony.

Left: A corridor with a vaulted window opening on to the new wing.

Above: The modern health club is situated under the roof of the building. Here there is little reference to the 17th century but rather a restrained grandeur reminiscent of the Baths of Caracalla in Rome. The pool is 6x11 metres and contains a counter-current facility.

Schlosshotel Vier Jahreszeiten

Berlin, Germany, 1994

Architecture: Hasso von Werder & Partner

Interior Design: Karl Lagerfeld/Ezra Attia Design, Julian Reed

THIS building is one of the last surviving examples of late-Wilhelminian villa architecture. The stately home was completed in 1914, just before Germany's pompous entry into a war which was to seal the fate of her empire; in its time this was the largest and most expensive private residence in Berlin, costing 5 million gold Marks to build. It was not just anyone who had decided to settle in the elegant Grünewald district: Walther von Pannwitz was the private legal adviser to Wilhelm II; he came from a wealthy Silesian aristocratic family and had increased his fortune by marriage. His royal client was the first visitor to this historicist palace, and is said to have admired the ostentatious architecture, hovering between the Renaissance and Baroque styles, and decorated with authentic works by Flemish masters. However, the splendour did not last long. When the Kaiser went into exile, von Pannwitz also withdrew from Germany's republican turmoil and emigrated to his Argentinian estates, where he died soon after. His widow did not live in Berlin and finally handed over the villa to the Nazi regime, which used it as an embassy for the favoured state of Croatia. When the Allies entered the city in 1945, the British took over the villa; finally in 1951 it was converted into a hotel. In this guise it welcomed more prominent guests, this time from the worlds of politics and showbusiness; Romy Schneider, the German film star, celebrated her two weddings here.

Four decades later, with the post-reunification boom in Berlin, the hotel saw the beginning of a new era. In 1992 the former Palais Pannwitz was acquired by investors who transformed it into the most exclusive top-class hotel in the country, a project that took three years and cost over DM35 million. Fashion designer Karl Lagerfeld was appointed as art director for the Schlosshotel Vier Jahreszeiten. Together with British interior design specialist Ezra Attia, he designed the luxurious interiors, right down to the last detail: 'Hôtel particulier is the French expression for an ideal home or the perfect town house. This hotel is an hôtel particulier in all the positive senses: individual, special, private and unique. I enjoy clothing a house. Every suite, every room must contribute to the harmonious whole. The house was to regain the original esprit. Nothing was left to chance, nothing remains anonymous: everything is personal. When you stay, I want you to feel that you are my personal guest' (Lagerfeld).

There were strict building conservation regulations to be observed, and Polish restorers were engaged for the meticulous renovation of the two-storey entrance hall and other original areas. The roof construction was modified to build two additional floors for guests. Altogether the hotel has 52 rooms and suites, two restaurants and bars. New additions include the glass bistro pavilion 'Le Jardin' and the health club with swimming pool. During excavations for the swimming pool (designed in a pseudo-Roman style) workers discovered another legacy of the old Berlin: an underground bunker from the Second World War. A little distance away under light pine trees is the new residential wing, intended as a home for long-staying guests. The hotel is opulently decorated, with countless antiques, exquisite silks and lavish crystal chandeliers. Lagerfeld's payment for his work on the project was unusual: he was given free use of his own suite in the hotel for the rest of his life. Mere paying mortals can also reside in this sanctuary – designed by Lagerfeld himself, of course – while the master is away.

Below: The late Prussian Berlin mansion was redecorated by Karl Lagerfeld as a homage to the classic *hôtel particulier*.

Opposite: The grand lobby of the Schlosshotel Vier Jahreszeiten.

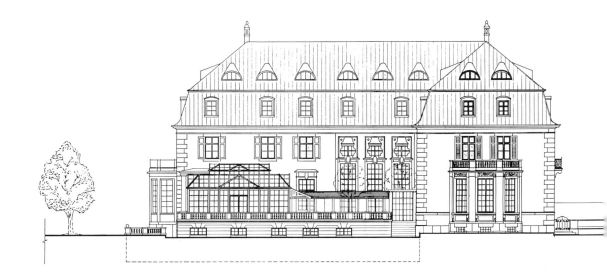

Right: Elevation of the hotel.

Below: Karl Lagerfeld's private suite was the substitute for the design fee. It can be rented by ordinary guests while the master of style is abroad.

Top right: The newly
added conservatory
houses the
bistro restaurant.

Right: The basement
pool and health
area invoke another
imperial style by
citing antique
Roman elements.

Hotel Costes

Paris, France, 1995

Architecture: Jacques Méchali

Interior Design: Jacques Garcia

JUST around the corner from the Ritz, a few steps from the Place Vendôme, the Restoration is in full swing. The Costes brothers, who once revolted against the sleepy Paris café culture of the mid-1980s, have now transformed themselves into latter-day admirers of the authoritarian, bourgeois emperor Napoleon III. In the 1980s, Jean-Louis and Gilbert Costes appointed 'enfant terrible' Philippe Starck to design their Café Costes, which became the first gastronomic mecca of modern design. A dozen years later and the café in the Marais has closed for ever, while the rebel Starck is earning himself a fortune with international projects from California to Bali. His one-time clients have changed their colours, selecting France's most accomplished nostalgia designer for their first excursion into the hotel sector. Jacques Garcia

is the darling of the beautiful, the rich, and the aristocratic, with clients including such illustrious figures as Princess Caroline of Monaco and Isabelle Adjani. He can create French castles in the Texan prairies or transform houses into Art Nouveau palaces on request. Or he can turn a rather battered hotel from the last century into a bourgeois luxury boudoir for the modern age. This is precisely what he has managed with the old Hotel France et Choiseul. 'We've done modern already. This time we wanted to go back into the past. I was longing to see this place transformed: it was to be a cross between a charming hotel and a palace. A mythical place' (Jean-Louis Costes).

In many respects the new retro-style hotel, simply called Hotel Costes, exudes more grandeur than its predecessor ever possessed. Inside the building was gutted and the old floor plans were eliminated in order to create space for larger rooms. Now the hotel has 85 rooms on six storeys and 4,890 square metres; on the ground floor around an intimate, classical-style *cour d'honneur* are the reception, bar, salons and a restaurant.

The Costes brothers played it safe in every respect. Architect Jacques Méchali had already built more than 5,000 hotel rooms in Paris, Garcia had designed not only exclusive private residences but also all the projects in the Lucien Barrière chain, including hotels in Enghien, Deauville and Cannes. In these projects a degree of standardization was required: in the Hotel Costes, by contrast, he had a free hand to make every room into an individual style experience. The sultry eclecticism of the Second Empire is skillfully re-created here, with its feast of historic and exotic borrowings. Genuine antiques, replicas, silk carpets in old patterns and the simple traditional patterns of Moroccan concrete tiles in the bathrooms: all combine to form an impressive, coherent work of art. The about-turn to conservative chic also seems to have pinpointed the mood of the times, just as the cool modern design of the Café did in the 1980s. Supermodels, Hollywood stars and Britpop celebrities have all chosen the Hotel Costes as their discreet *pied-à-terre* in the French capital.

Above: The bedrooms have the atmosphere
of an intimate apartment. Garcia has
himself indulged in different tones of red
and rich materials.

Opposite: The inner courtyard was redone
in perfect neoclassical style.

The restaurant recreates, with
columns and wall mirrors, the fine
hospitality of *fin-de-siècle* dining.

Above left: Club style lobby seating.

**Above right: The courtyard
conservatory with bistro tables.**

ARCHITECTS AND INTERIOR DESIGNERS

ABACUS DESIGN CO. LTD.
144 Sukhumvit 81, Suanluang,
Bangkok 10250, Thailand
Headed by principal Partners, Mr John D.
Lightbody and Mrs M. L. Lightbody, Abacus
Design was founded in 1976 and today is
one of Thailand's leading interior design
companies, specializing in hotels, resorts
and restaurants. Projects include the Regent
Chiang Mai Resort (which was awarded the
1997 Asia-Pacific Interior Design Prize);
the Westin Chiangmai; the Royal Cliff Grand
and the Abacus Residence.

AIC
Sauerlacher Strasse 64,
82041 Deisenhofen, Germany
AIC offers a full range of architectural
services. Their main areas of activity include
offices and administrative buildings, hotels
and restaurants, residential buildings,
conversions and restorations, residential
homes and care facilities. Major projects
include the Grand Hotel 'Adlon', Berlin; the
Grand Hotel 'Kempinski' in Budapest; The
Taschenbergpalais in Dresden; administrative
and research building in Soeenheim; The
Max Reinhardt Centre in Berlin; the
preliminary plans for the
Wintergartenquartier in Friedrichstrasse in
Berlin and the Wohnpark Sterntaler, Potsdam
(residential park of 244 units plus
underground car parking).

ASHIHARA ARCHITECT AND ASSOCIATES
7th Floor, Sumitomo Seimei Building,
31-15 Sakuragaoka-cho, Shibuya-ku,
Tokyo 150, Japan
Yoshinobu Ashihara established his own
company in 1956 and today employs over 40
staff. Projects completed include the
Phoenix Resort (Seagaia); the Tokyo
Metropolitan Art Space; National Museum of
Japanese History; the Sony Building; the
Komazawa Olympic Gymnasium and Control
Tower; and the Japanese Pavilion for the
International Exposition in Montreal 1967.
He was born in Tokyo in 1918 and graduated
from the University of Tokyo in 1942. He
pursued his architectural studies at the
Harvard School of Design but eventually
received his doctorate from Tokyo Univ. in
1962 where today he is Professor Emeritus.
He served as President of the Japan
Architects Association and also of the
Architectural Institute of Japan.

AUT-DESIGN
Lutticher Str 281,
D52074 Aachen, Germany
AUT-Design was founded by Harald Klein in
1985 after completion of his photographic
studies and further training in art and
interior design at the college in Aachen.
Main areas of activity have always been
hotels, restaurants, shops offices and private
apartments. Klein has collaborated with
Seidler Hotels since 1991 working on
numerous building for them. In 1993 Bert
Haller joined the company as interior
architect and partner. Projects to date
include Bar 'Telekom Lounge airport,
Frankfurt; the Einhorn pharmacy, Duisberg;
a marina in Berlin; a gallery and house for
Dr. Mayerl and the Belvedere restaurant
in Berlin.

ARGE BAUMSCHLAGER-EBERLE
Lindauerstrasse 31,
A-6911 Lochau, Austria
Baumschlager-Eberle-Eger was founded in

1984 becoming just Baumschlager-Eberle the
following year. Carlo Baumschlager was born
in 1956. He studied at the School of Applied
Arts in Vienna before taking a course in
industrial design under Hans Hollein. From
1978-82 he trained as an architect with
Prof. W. Holzbauer and Prof. Ungers. He was
made Professor at Syracuse University, New
York in 1994. Dietmar Eberle (b. 1952) was
educated at the Technical University in
Vienna from which he graduated in 1978
receiving his Diploma from Prof.
Schweighofer. He worked on town-planning
research in Iran in the 70s before joining
Cooperative Bauplanungs GmbH where he
remained until he started his collaboration
with Baumschlager. He has taught at the
Technical Universities of Hanover and Vienna
and has been Professor of visual design at
the Hochschule, Linz, and at the ETH in
Zürich. In 1994 he was Professor at Syracuse
University, New York along with his partner.

BARTO + BARTO
23 rue Chezine,
44100 Nantes, France
Bernard Barto was born in 1937 in Nantes.
He studied fine art at the Beaux-Arts de
Nantes and later at the Beaux Arts in Paris.
He founded his own practice in the late 60s
and has taught architecture in Nantes since
1977. His partner, Clotilde Barto, was born
in 1948 and studied psychology in Rennes.
Their early works included mural painting,
sculpture and graphic design, disciplines
with which they are still involved today. In
the 80s they became interested in urban
planning executing plans for the Ile
Beaulieu, Nantes and the Parc de la Villette
in Paris. They completed schemes such as
the tramway lines in Nantes (1980) and the
Place des Thebauldieres in Saint-Herblain.
Notable architectural projects are the Cinema
'Concerde' at La Roche-sur-Yon (1977); the
central bus station in Nantes (1980); Maison
Chezine, Nantes (1983); the Audi-Volkswagen
garage in Nantes (1988); and La Pérouse
hotel in Nantes.

MARIANNE BURKHALTER + CHRISTIAN SUMI ARCHITEKTEN
Munstergasse 18a, 8001 Zürich,
Switzerland
Marianne Burkhalter was trained as technical
draughtswoman in the office of Hubacher
and Issler in Zürich and spent two years at
Princeton University in 1973-5. Until her
collaboration with Christian Sumi in 1984
she worked for several architectural practices
in Switzerland, Florence, New York and Los
Angeles. From 1981-83 she assisted Prof
Klaus Vogt at the ETH in Zürich and Prof
Mario Campi the following year. She has
been a guest professor at SCIARC in Los
Angeles and from 1990 has been a member
of the Commission on the Cityscape in
Baden. Christian Sumi was born in 1950 and
received an architectural diploma from the
ETH in Zürich. In 1978-81 he worked at the
German Archaeological Institute in Rome
after which he became a research fellow at
the Institute for History and Theory of
Architecture. He was guest professor at the
School of architecture at the University
of Geneva and at Harvard University. Recent
architectural schemes include two forest
stations in Turbenthal and Rheinau; a
kindergarten in Lustenau and the Hotel
Zürichberg. They are currently working on
the Hotel Dorinth in Weimar; the Anbau
Restaurant in Tierpark and the restoration
Empa in Dubendorf.

JOAO LUÍS CARRILHO DA GRAÇA
Calçada Marques de Abrantes 48,
1200 Lisbon, Portugal
Joao Luís Carrilho da Graça was born in
Portalegre in 1952 and graduated from
ESBAL (the College of Fine Arts) in 1977. He
has run his own architectural practice since
that time and has received much acclaim
within his native country. He was nominated
for the Mies Van der Rohe European
Architecture Award in 1991,92,94 and 1996
and in 1992 received the AICA/SEC
(International Art Critics
Association/Portuguese Cultural Department)
Award. From 1987 to 1992 he was Associate
Professor at the College of Architecture
in Lisbon.

JOSE MARIA CARTAÑA
Teodora Lamadrid 8-10, 08022
Barcelona, Spain
Cartañá graduated as an architect from the
Escuela Tecnica Superior de Arquitectos de
Barcelona in 1976. Since the early 90s he
has carried out major residential projects in
France and Spain as well as work on the
Olympic village of Valle Hebron where he
was responsible for the creation of over 510
flats, commercial areas and parking lots.
In 1988-92 he was involved with Carlos
Ferrater in the four-star luxury hotel Juan
Carlos and has since added a health spa to
the site.

CD PARTNERSHIP
22 Shad Thames, London,
SE1 2YU, Great Britain
The architecture, interior and graphic design
practice, CD Partnership, was founded by
Terence Conran and today employs over 20
designers and architects. Current projects
include the design of the Longman
Publishing Group's new headquarters in
Harlow, Essex; the Conran restaurant Mezzo;
the café and lido on two levels of Celebrity
Cruises' new super liner launched in 1995;
The Triest Hotel in Vienna; Selfridges'
restaurant; and Quaglinos restaurant in
London. Graphic projects include the full
design and implementation of the new
corporate identity for Cabouchon, the UK's
leading fashion jeweller, and a development
programme for Providence Capitol's product
literature.

CHIANGMAI ARCHITECTS COLLABORATIVE
50 Rachadammern Road
Chiangmai, Thailand
Chiangmai Collaborative was founded by
Chulathat Kitibutr (b. 1944) and graduated
from Chulalongkorn University in Bangkok in
1970. He returned to Chiangmai and taught
at the Northern Technical School as well as
establishing his own firm. He was a visiting
lecturer at the Department of Landscape
Design from 1985-87 and in the Department
of Architecture since 1995. He has designed
several buildings including private
residences, temples and resorts respecting
the northern Thai tradition or 'Lanna' Style.
Recent work includes the Khun Surai House,
the Napadoi, the Wat Analayo temple and
residence, the Huahin Royal Garden Village
resort and the Regent Resort, Chiangmai. In
1996 he was the recipient of the Heritage
Preservation Award.

COSTELLO MURRAY BEAUMONT
7 St Stephens Green,
Dublin 2, Ireland
Costello Murray Beaumont (CMB) was

founded in 1970 when two firms, Murray and
Beaumont and John Costello and Associates
merged. CMB Design was added to the
practice in 1990 and the company is now
active in all fields of architectural design as
well as office/space planning, interior
design and graphics. Recent projects include
the Four Courts, Dublin; the Clarence Hotel,
Dublin; the Irish Life Centre, Dublin; the
Irish Management Institute, Sandyford; the
Public Records Office in Dublin and the
Hibernian Way. They are frequent recipients
of awards from the RIAI.

DENTON CORKER MARSHALL
49 Exhibition Street, Melbourne,
Victoria 3000, Australia
Denton Corker Marshall was founded in
Melbourne in 1972 and today has offices in
Sydney, Hong Kong, Jakarta, Singapore, Ho
Chi Minh City, London and Warsaw. They are
involved in architecture, landscape design,
planning, exhibition and interior design, and
project management. They work on all scales
from small domestic schemes to major urban
developments and have received
international acclaim for their projects,
attracting important corporate clients and
government bodies. The practice has
received numerous prizes and is the subject
of a major new monograph published by the
RAIA. John Denton, Bill Corker and Barrie
Marshall were jointly awarded the Royal
Australian Institute of Architects Gold Medal
in 1996.

DIVISION Y DISENO DE INTERIORES (DDI)
(no longer in existence)

ANDREW DOOLAN ARCHITECTS
34 Bread Street, Edinburgh,
EH3 9AF, Great Britain
Andrew Doolan was born in Glasgow in
1951 and studied at Leeds School of
Architecture from 1970-76. He founded the
Kantel group of companies including
Andrew Doolan Architects in 1980. The
Kantel group also includes funding,
construction and management companies.
Kantel owns and operates the Point Hotel
and was responsible for its design and
construction. Andrew Doolan has worked
mainly in Scotland and his holistic approach
to projects has enabled him to build many
substantial buildings in Scotland. His
approach to design is minimalist and
colourful and through his innovative use of
light and glass he brings excitement to
his buildings.

DORINE DE VOS
c/o Hotel New York,
Koninginnenhoofd No. 1,
3072 AD Rotterdam,
The Netherlands
Dorine de Vos was the art director
responsible for the Hotel New York she
was responsible for the coordination of
the scheme as well as the graphic and
interior design.

PAUL DRAPER AND ASSOCIATES
416 Swiss Avenue, Dallas,
Texas 75204, USA
Paul Draper and Associates are an
established interior design company
specialising in restaurant and hotel schemes.
They are responsible for the Sfuzzi chain of
restaurants with branches throughout the
USA. Their work has been widely published
in the national press.

ECART
111 rue Saint-Antoine,
75004 Paris, France
Ecart was founded in 1978 by Andrée Putman (who left the company in 1997). Putman was born in Paris and studied music under Poulenc, before becoming first a journalist and later a design consultant for the mass-market chain Prisunic, and then co-founder of 'Createurs et Industriels', which introduced the work of Issey Miyake and Jean Muir, among others, to France. The Ecart practice is divided into three specific disciplines. Ecart SA, specialises in interior and product design, varying from hotels to boutiques, corporate offices to private houses and museums to governmental offices. Notable designs include the Office of the Minister of Culture (1984), Ebel Headquarters (1985), Morgans Hotel (1985), and the Im Wasserturm Hotel (1990). Ecart Internations re-works furniture and objects by such designers as Eileen Gray and Mariano Fortuny and designs by Ecart SA (designers regularly used include Patrick Naggar, Paul Mathieu and Michael Ray). The Andrée Putman licensing division designs objects distributed throughout the world, which include rugs, upholstery fabrics, tableware and bathroom accessories.

ELDER AND CANNON ARCHITECTS
551 Sauchiehall Street,
Glasgow, G3 7PQ, Great Britain
Elder and Cannon was founded in 1980 and early projects included two sites for the National Bank of Pakistan, one in London and the other in Glasgow, the D and D Warehouse, and the Church of the Holy Name. In 1984 the practice was chosen to design Ingram Square in Glasgow, the first phase in the rejuvenation of the merchant area of the city. The Duke Street Residential and Commercial Development for Reidvale Housing Association in the east end of Glasgow won both the Saltire Award and the GIA Design Award and was instrumental in Glasgow's successful bid for the 1999 Year of Architecture and Design. They have recently completed the Annandale Square residential development, a modern infill scheme on the fourth side of a Victorian square. Elder and Cannon are also active in hotel design, conversions and community architecture. In 1996 they were one of the finalists in the international competition for the National Museum and Gallery of Scotland and they have recently been awarded the Regeneration Design Prize for the Brunswick Hotel from the Scottish Enterprise Board.

EZRA ATTIA DESIGN
3 Belsize Place,
London, NW3 5AL, Great Britain
EAA International was founded in 1979 and specialises in space planning, architecture, interior design and procurement for the hotel and leisure industry. Today they have offices in London, Berlin, Istanbul, Israel and Abu Dhabi and clients include such names as Crest Hotels, Garrard & Co. Crown Jewellers, Hilton International, Gleneagles Hotel, Holiday Inn, Hyatt, Hilton, Kempinski, ITT Sheraton, Thistle Hotels, Trusthouse Forte and Westin. The practice has worked on hotels throughout the world.

CARLOS FERRATER
C/Bertran 67 Bjos
08023 Barcelona, Spain.
Carlos Ferrater was born in Barcelona in 1944. He qualified as an architect from the Architecture School of Barcelona in 1971 since when he has run his own practice, being joined by Joan Guibernau in 1993. Recent projects include the Hotel Rey Juan Carlos 1 and Fitness Centre with J. M. Cartañá, Headquarters of the Consell Comarcal del Baix Lobregat with X Guell and Headquarters for the Research Centre in Castellon with J. Sanahuja and C. Bento. He has been involved with the Architecture School in Barcelona since 1971 and has held a permanent position since 1987. He was also the Director of the Architecture course at the Menendez Pelayo International University in Santander and President of the ADI-FAD, INFAD and ARQ-INFAD between 1985 and 1992. In 1995 he was made Director of the IV Biennial Spanish Architecture. Ferrater's work has received many national awards most recently the Mies van der Rohe Award in 1992 for the Yacht Club in Estartit and in 1996 for the IMPIVA headquarters.

GAPP
97 Second Avenue Melville 2092,
PO Box 31133, Braamfontein 2017,
Cape Town, South Africa
Gapp Architects and City Planners are active in a wide range of architectural activities from city centre strategies and urban regeneration, restoration of historical buildings and precincts to the design of offices and office parks, cultural facilities, resorts, hotels, housing, industrial buildings, waterfronts and marinas.

JACQUES GARCIA
239 rue St Honoré
75001 Paris, France
Jacques Garcia was born in 1947 and trained in the 'Penningen Workshops'. During his early career he specialised in contemporary architecture and was responsible for the interiors of the Montparnasse Tower and the Meridien and Sofitel hotels. Today his work is influenced by the past, integrating clients' 'objets d'art' into an environment which both defines the spirit of an era while avoiding a museum style concept. His projects include various domestic interiors as well as the corporate design of the Lucien Barriere chain of hotels; the Strasburger Museum and the recreation of the Chateau du Champ sur Marne in Houston, Texas. In 1995 Garcia undertook the renovation of the France and Choiseul hotel in Paris and the following year overhauled the design concept for Mauboussin's chain of jewellery boutiques. Other recent projects include the renovation of the restaurant and night club 'La Villa Barclays' and of the 'Japan Grill' in Paris.

GASKIN & BEZANSKI ARCHITECTURE AND ENGINEERING
3430 East Flamingo, Suite 232,
Las Vegas, NV 89121, USA
Gaskin and Bezanski Inc. is a leading architectural and structural engineering firm based in Las Vegas and specialising in the hotel/casino/hospitality industry. The practice was founded in 1976 by F. Neal Gaskin Jr. architect who has been designing projects throughout the Southwest since 1970 and structural engineer Ilia M. Bezanski who has been working since 1972. Major hotel schemes include Caesars Palace, Casino Royale, Gold Strike, Riverside and Palace Station. They have also worked on residential developments, modern shopping centres, office buildings and exotic gambling casinos such as New York New York

COLIN GOLD
4 Masters Lodge, Johnson Street,
London, E1 OBE, Great Britain
Colin Gold trained at the Chartered Society of Designers and worked for Aukett Associates as Design/Creative director before founding his own consultancy in 1993. Since this time he has been working on a freelance basis for clients such as Areen Design Services. He also joined Richmond International for a short period to head the design team responsible for the competition project for the Grand Adlon Hotel in Berlin. He has carried out office, retail, restaurant and domestic design throughout the UK as well as in Europe, Israel, Saudi Arabia and China. His work has been published in many leading design journals

GRAVEN IMAGES
83a Candleriggs,
Glasgow, Great Britain
Graven Images was established in 1986 by Ross Hunter and Janice Kirkpatrick as a multi-disciplinary consultancy. They are active in the fields of graphic design, interior and exhibition design, furniture and product design. Projects include the Brunswick Hotel in Edinburgh, the Indigo Yard restaurant and bar also in Edinburgh and Habitat in Norwich. Exhibitions recently completed include the major UK style show for the Department of Trade and Industry which will travel to Korea, New Zealand and Hong Kong in 1997. Janice Kirkpatrick is a visiting lecturer in Product Design at Glasgow School of Art and Design and was awarded the prestigious title of 'Collector' for the Conran Foundation Archive in 1996.

MICHAEL GRAVES
341 Nassau Street, Princeton,
New Jersey 08540, USA
Michael Graves was born in Indianapolis and received his architectural training at the universities of Cincinnati and Harvard. Since the formation of his practice in 1964 he has been in partly responsible for moving urban architecture away from abstract Modernism towards more contextual and traditional themes. Through his affiliated company Graves Design he has produced an extensive collection of furniture and consumer products, collaborating with manufacturers such as Alessi, Arkitektura, Swid Powell, Baldinger and Atelier International. Major architectural projects include the Walt Disney World Swan and Dolphin Hotels, Orlando, Florida; The Disney Company Corporate Headquarters Burbank, California; The Crown American Offices; the Whitney Museum of American Art in Johnstown; a master plan for the Detroit Institute of Arts; the Denver Public Library and the Clark County Library in Las Vegas. Graves has designed the Life 1996 Dream House and has recently been selected as the principal designer of the US Courthouse Annex in Washington, DC. He is a member of the American Institute of Architects and has received many awards and nine American Institute of Architects National Honour Awards. Graves is the Schirmer Professor of Architecture at Princeton University, where he has taught since 1962.

GUYMER BAILEY ARCHITECTS
47 Anderson Street, Fortitude Valley
Brisbane, 4006, Australia
Guymer Bailey was founded by Brisbane-based architect Tim Guymer and Ralph Bailey who was the former supervising architect with the State Government's Department of Works with the specific purpose of designing a resort and village at Kingfisher Bay on Fraser Island. Since this time they have completed several commercial projects, prisons, community facilities, Brisbane's South Bank 'Gondwana Rainforest Sanctuary' and numerous residences. The practice recently received the HIA Award for the best home in the $200,000 to $300,000 category for the Beitz residence in Chapel Hill.

HELPERN ARCHITECTS
23 East 4th Street, New York,
New York 10003, USA
Helpern Architects was set up over 25 years ago and their commissions range in scale and scope from new constructions to historic restoration and adaptive reuse and from expansion of existing buildings to masterplanning. Current clients include the University of Pennsylvania (creation of 'The Penn Club' dining catering and hotel facilities); The Starwood Lodging Corporation (expansion of the Doral Inn); Hartz Mountain (award-winning high rise office building and new building design for the Soho Grand, both in New York); and New York University (campus facilities master plan, Centre building for the Stern School of Business and a masterplan to create a new centre of undergraduate life in the main building). The practice is a frequent recipient of major national design awards most notably from from the AIA and was recently honoured by the Municipal Art Society for Historic Preservation for work carried out on the Penn Club and by the Art Commission of the City of New York for the design of the Congo Forest Exhibit and Education Centre at the Bronx Zoo which is due to open in 1999.

ANOUSKA HEMPEL DESIGNS
c/o The Hempel,
31-35 Craven Hill Gardens,
London, W2 3EA, Great Britain
Anouska Hempel's major design projects to date include Blakes Hotel, London, 1985; Anouksa Hempel Couture shop, London, 1989; BSkyB Television Headquarters, London, 1993; 10 berth Turkish Gulet, 1995-6; Louis Vuitton shop, Paris, 1996; The Hempel Hotel and garden square, London, 1996; and the Louis Vuitton pen range, 1997 as well as various private residences. In 1990 she was awarded the Designers Accolade from the Fashion Group International and her fashion designs have been on show at the Victoria and Albert Museum in London. Current projects include Blakes hotel in Amsterdam, New York and Singapore and a major urban development in Calcutta.

HILL GLAZIER ARCHITECTS INC.
700 Welch Road, Palo Alto,
California 94304, USA
Hill Glazier Architects was founded in 1980 since which time it has built up extensive experience in the design of specialty stores, international resorts, hotels, restaurants, conference centres and commercial and office buildings. They have received wide acclaim for their respect of historical traditions, the natural environment and the aesthetic concerns of the project's community. The firm has received numerous and prestigious national and international awards and has been featured in a wide variety of national and international publications.

HIRSCH BEDNER ASSOCIATES

909 W. Peachtree Street,
Atlanta, GA, USA

Founded in 1964 under the name of Howard Hirsch and Associates, the practice has gained an international reputation in hotel and restaurant design. Michael Bedner has been employed by the company since the beginning, to become full partner and CEO of the company. Today the practice has offices in Hong Kong, Atlanta, London, Singapore, San Francisco and Sydney. The London branch which opened in 1987 has completed major projects throughout Europe while the Atlanta office opened in 1980 works mainly in the USA, Caribbean, Latin America, Middle East, Africa, Canada, Asia and Australia. Clients include Hyatt Hotel Corporation, Ritz-Carlton Hotel Company, ITT Sheraton, Renaissance, Hilton Hotels and Swissair. Recent projects include The Park Lane Hotel, London, the Hyatt Regency, Roissy, the Aqaba Bridge Movenpick Hotel, Jordan, Conrad Jakarta, the Gloucester, London and the Hyatt Regency Cebu, Mactan Island, Philippines

BARBARA HULANICKI

c/o Island Outpost Inc., The
Netherland, 1330 Ocean Drive,
Miami Beach, FL 33139, USA

Barbara Hulanicki made her name in the 60s with the design of Biba in London. She is presently involved in the design of a string of hotels for Island Outposts.

FRIEDENSREICH HUNDERTWASSER

Joram Harel, Gesellschaft mit
Beschraukter, Hattung,
P.O. Box 28, Vienna

Friedensreich Hundertwasser was born in Vienna in 1928 as Friedrich Stowasser. After graduating from the 'realgymnasium' he spent three months at the Academy of Fine Arts in Vienna. In 1949 he met René Bro and moved with him to Paris. Here he began to develop his idiosyncratic style and changed his name to Hundertwasser. In the 1970s he began his collaboration with Joram Horel which was to lead eventually to his series of architectural projects starting with the Hundertwasser House in Vienna. In 1981 he was awarded the Grand Austrian State Prize and gave a speech against nuclear power and on 'Wrong Art'. During the same year he delivered a series of lectures on environment, architecture and art throughout Germany and Austria. He was also appointed head of the master painting class at the Academy of Fine Arts in Vienna. The 90s have seen Hundertwasser concentrating on his building schemes. Completed architectural projects include the Rosenthal Factory, Selb; the Church of St Barbara, Barnbach; the 'In the Meadows' housing project, Bad Soden; the Day-care Centre in Heddernheim; and the Blumau Hot Springs Village.

FRANKLIN D. ISRAEL DESIGN ASSOCIATES

Israel Callas Shortridge Ass Inc
254 So Robertson Blvd,
Suite 205, Beverly Hills,
CA 90211, USA

Franklin D. Israel Associates was founded in 1983. Israel was educated at Penn, Yale and Columbia universities and before setting up his own practice worked for various architects in New York, London and Tehran. His major schemes include the corporate headquarters for Virgin Records in Beverly Hills; the Weisman Art Pavilion and Foundation offices in Beverly Hills; the Malibu beach house of Mr and Mrs Robert Altman; the offices of Propaganda Films in Hollywood and Tisch/Avnet Production in Culver City. In 1992 Rizzoli published a monograph on Israel's work. Before his death, he was Associate Professor at the School of Architecture and Urban Planning at UCLA.

KISHO KUROKAWA ARCHITECT AND ASSOCIATES

11F Aoyama Bldg,
1-2-3 Kita Aoyama, Minato-ku,
Tokyo 107, Japan

Kisho Kurokawa was born in Nagoya in 1934 and studied architecture at Kyoto University. In 1960, while studying for a doctorate at Tokyo University, he formed the Metabolist Group, whose philosophy – closely linked with Buddhism – viewed urban architectural forms as organisms capable of growth and change, a belief which is echoed in his designs to date, most notably: the capsule pavilions at the International Expo 1970, Osaka; the Nagakin Capsule Tower, Tokyo (1972); and Sony Tower, Osaka (1976). Major projects include: The National Bunraku Theatre, Osaka; the Roppongi Prince Hotel, Tokyo; the Japanese-German Culture Centre in Berlin and the National Museums of Modern Art in Nagoya, Hiroshima and Wakayama. He has also designed distinctive furniture for Tnedo and Kosuga. Kurokawa is a member of the Japan Institute of Architects and an Honorary Fellow of both the American Institute of Architects and an Honorary Fellow of both the American Institute of Architects and the Royal Institute of British Architects. He has been awarded the Japan Grand Prize and citations of excellence from the AIA for his 'Philosophy of Symbiosis' in 1992. In 1993 he was presented with the Deutschen Naturstein-Preis for the Japanese-German Centre in Berlin.

KARL LAGERFELD

c/o Schlosshotel Vier Jahreszeiten

Karl Lagerfeld was born in Hamburg in 1938. At the age of 15 he went to Paris and won first prize in a coat design competition. Two years later he became assistant to Pierre Balmain and later artistic director at Jean Patou where he stayed until 1963. Since that date he has been an independent fashion designer working in France, Italy, Germany and Japan working for clients such as Fendi, Chloe and Dunhill. He launched his perfume range in 1974 and in 1983 began working with Chanel as artistic director of *haute couture*, designing 5 collections per year. From 1984-97 he has produced his own ready-to-wear and accessories collection for women, Karl Lagerfeld SA. Lagerfeld has designed clothes for cinema and opera. In 1987 he started his parallel career as a photographer.

AB 'LIVING DESIGNS'

PO Box 142, S-182
05 Djursholm, Sweden

Living Designs was founded in 1983 and today is one of Europe's leading interior design companies involved in the hospitality industry. They are involved from space planning through design to furniture purchasing, installation, art selection and hand-over. The practice has completed over 80 projects during the last 10 years including the Grand Hotel Europe in St Petersburg, the Grand Hotel Kempinski Corvinius in Budapest, the Holiday Inn Crown Plaza in Amsterdam, the Taschenbergpalais Hotel Kempinski in Dresden, the Bristol Hotel Kempinski in Berlin, the Grand Hotel Adlon in Berlin and the Grand Hotel in Stockholm

JACQUES MÉCHALI

42 rue du Dr Roux,
75015 Paris, France

Cabinet Méchali was founded in 1976 by Jacques Méchali. He graduated from the Ecole des Beaux Arts in Paris where he studied architecture and was incorporated into the French National Order of architects in 1996. Méchali specialises in the restoration of Paris' *fin-de-siècle* buildings and to date has worked on over 45 projects including the historic Trianon Palace Hotel in the gardens of the Palace of Versailles and the Hotel Costes.

METEX DESIGN GROUP

Barbaros Bulvari Murbassan Sok, Koza is
Meikezi, B Blok Kat, 7 Balmumcu-Besiktas,
Istanbul, Turkey

Metex Design Group was founded in 1991 by Kafadar and Cavit Sarioglu. Kafadar was born in 1964 in Istanbul and graduated from the Architectural Faculty of Istanbul Technical University in 1986. After working and studying in London, Montreal and Rome for 4 years, he returned to Istanbul where he now practises architecture and interior design.

FRANCO MIRENZI (UNIMARK)

Via Revere 9,
20123 Milan, Italy

Franco Mirenzi studied in Venice and worked for Angelo Mangiarotti until he started his collaboration with Unimark International in 1967. He has worked for clients such as Rank Xerox, Zanussi and Fiat Componenti as well as for the hotel chain Forte Crest. He has twice been recognised by the Compasso d'Oro and has been active in various noteworthy exhibitions such as the 'Design e Design' with a specially equipped wall for Citterio and 'Le Torri della Luce' a permanent installation for Fidenza Vetrarie and Comune di Milano. In 1986 he was awarded the Smau prize for a telephone apparatus designed for Telettra and in 1995 he designed the interiors of the Hotel Méridien in Lingotto, Turin, in association with Renzo Piano.

MORFORD & COMPANY LTD.

5/F 8-10 On Lan Street,
Central Hong Kong

John Morford obtained a Bachelor of Architecture from the University of Notre Dame in the USA in 1963, a Masters from Rice University two years later and attended the Academy of Fine Arts in Rome from 1965-6. He has had his own company since 1984 before which he worked in various practices in the States, Rome, Paris and Hong Kong. He specialises in hotel and restaurant design, and recently completed projects include the Han Residence in Bangkok; the Park Hyatt in Tokyo; the Grand Hyatts in Seoul, Berlin and Hong Kong; the Joyce Café, Nathan Road, Hong Kong; and the Joyce Café, Exchange Square also in Hong Kong.

JASPER MORRISON

43 Charterhouse Square
London, EC1M 6EA, Great Britain

Jasper Morrison was born in London in 1959 and studied at the Kingston School of Art and the Royal College of Art, winning a Berlin scholarship in 1984. In 1986 he established his own design office in London. He designs for SCP, Cappellini and Vitra, and lectures at the Hochschule der Kunste, Berlin and Saarbrucken, the European Institute of Design, Milan and the Royal College of Art, London. He has exhibited widely in Europe and the UK.

MURPHY/JAHN INC.

35 East Wacker Drive,
Chicago, Illinois 60601, USA

The original firm was founded over 50 years ago since which time, Helmut Jahn, President and Chief Executive Officer, has built up a considerable reputation, his buildings having received numerous design awards. The practice has offices in the USA, Berlin and Munich. They serve a broad spectrum of private, corporate, institutional and governmental clients, and their large high-rise and commercial structures have been frequently published by the international press. The American Institute of Architects wrote 'With incredible energy, Helmut Jahn has explored alternatives to Modernism in a wilful and romantic direction that few large-scale commercial buildings can surpass. His highly exciting vision has left a bold imprint on architecture worldwide'.

DIETER NEIKES

Architektur Neikes, Pelikanstr. 7,
D-30177 Hanover, Germany

Dieter Neikes was born in Monchengladbach in 1955. He studied architectural and technical drawing before graduating as an architect from Aachen Technical College in 1980. He founded his own practice, Architektur Neikes in 1983. In 1987 he was made a member of the BDA and later worked at the Fachhochschule in Aachen. He is a member of the chamber of architects in both Nordrhein-Westfalen and Niedersachsen. His company has a second branch in Hanover. In 1994 Neikes also opened a project management and design office which carries out design projects, including projects for Kreon-Lights, furniture, building extensions and advertising plans.

YALÇIN ÖZÜEKREN

Tevfik Erdönmez Sok. No. 26/11
Dikt Apt., Esentere 80280, Sisli,
Istanbul, Turkey

Yalçin Özüekren was born in 1948 and graduated from the Lycée Saint Joseph in 1968. He studied architecture at the Faculty of Architecture, Istanbul Technical University and graduated in 1974. He received his PhD in 1982 and worked as assistant professor in the same faculty from 1975 to 1983 where he specialised in renovation. He founded his own company, Kovuk, in 1983 which now includes an architectural design office, a wood workshop producing building components and a construction team. He works mainly on the renovation of Turkish wooden houses and he has been nominated for the Aga Khan Award in Architecture for the restoration of the Hisar House at Bosporus in Istanbul.

PEI COBB FREED & PARTNERS

600 Madison Avenue, New York,
NY 10022, USA

Ieoh Ming Pei was born in China in 1917. He moved to the USA to study architecture at the Massachusetts Institute of Technology, receiving a Bachelor of Architecture degree in 1940. He then studied at the Harvard Graduate School of Design under Walter Gropius, at the same time teaching in the faculty as Assistant Professor, and gained a Master's degree in 1946. In 1955, Pei formed I.M. Pei & Associates, which became I.M. Pei and Partners in 1966 and Pei Cobb Freed and Partners in 1989. The practice has designed over 150 projects in the USA and abroad, more that half of which have won awards and citations. As well as working for corporate and private investment clients, the practice has executed numerous commissions for public authorities and religious, educational and cultural institutions. Its most important buildings include the Bank of China, Hong Kong; the East West Wing of the National Gallery of Washington DC; the Grand Louvre in Paris; and the United States Holocaust Memorial Museum, Washington. Works recently completed are the Federal Triangle, Washington, and the San Francisco Main Public Library. Pei is a Fellow of the American Institute of Architects, a Corporate Member of the Royal Institute of British Architects and in 1975 he was made a Member of the American Academy. James Ingo Freed was the design architect for the San Francisco Public Library and is one of the three design principals of Pei Cobb Freed. He joined the offices in 1956, before which he worked in Chicago and New York, notably in the office of Mies van der Rohe. He received his architectural degree from the Illinois Institute of Technology and has received more than one hundred major awards including, most recently, the National Endowment for the Arts' National Medal of arts, which was conferred by President Clinton in 1995.

PETER PELIKAN
Lainzerstr 10,
1130 Vienna, Austria
Peter Pelikan was born in 1941 in Austria. He studied architecture in Vienna and worked for the city after his graduation. His cooperation with Hundertwasser started in 1981 with the Hundertwasserhaus and he has been working freelance since 1989.

CESAR PELLI AND ASSOCIATES INC.
1056 Chapel Street,
New Haven,
CT. 06510, USA
Cesar Pelli founded his own company in 1977, after a career which had seen, amongst other projects, the construction of the Pacific Design Centre in Los Angeles and the US Embassy in Tokyo, and his appointment as Dean of the Yale University of School of Architecture. Born in Argentina, and trained at the University of Tucuman, Pelli came to the USA with a scholarship to attend the University of Illinois. His belief that buildings should be 'responsible citizens' is reflected in his concern for their suitability in terms of locations and the city skyline. His first project after 1977 was the expansion and renovation of the Museum of Modern Art in New York, since which time the company has been the recipient of over eighty awards for design excellence, including an AIA citation for the World Financial Centre and Winter Garden at Battery Park City, which they cited as being one of the ten best works of architecture completed after 1980. The AIA also awarded Cesar Pelli and Associate the 1989 Firm Award, in recognition of over a decade of leading-edge work in architectural design.

Most recently Pelli himself was given the AIA 1995 Gold Medal which honours a lifetime of distinguished achievements and outstanding contributions.

RENZO PIANO
via P.P. Rubens 29,
16158 Genova, Italy
Renzo Piano was born in Genoa in 1937 and graduated from from the School of Architecture at Milan Polytechnic in 1964. He worked with Louis Kahn in Philadelphia and Z. S. Malowski in London, before collaborating with Richard Rogers, Peter Rice and Richard Fitzgerald. In 1981 he established the Renzo Piano Building Workshop and today has offices in Genoa, Paris and Osaka. Recent projects include the Kansai International Airport, the Potsdamer Platz Urban Redevelopment, Cité Internationale in Lyons, the Science and Technology Museum in Amsterdam and the Mercedes Benz offices in Stuttgart.

ILAN PIVKO ARCHITECT
23 Hatzedef Street,
Jaffa 68034, Israel
Ilan Pivko is a graduate from the faculty of architecture of the Technion, Haifa. Since his graduation he has specialised in the planning of residential buildings in Tel Aviv and Yaffo and has also completed various public buildings and hotels.

PMG ARCHITECTS
156 Fifth Avenue, New York,
NY 10010, USA
PMG was established in 1992 by Peter Michael Gumpel. A graduate of the Harvard University Graduate School of Design, he has experience in virtually every building type. The practice specialises in renovation, restoration and rehabilitation of buildings with emphasis on the hospitality industry and has just completed the renovation of the Delano Hotel in Miami. PMG's have received a number of awards including the AIA Building Award, Interiors Award and two Awards of Merit and has also appeared in all the major professional journals. Important schemes include hotels and housing projects in New York and New Jersey, Columbia University, Ferris Booth Hall Conversion in New York, the De Vry Institute and Technology building in Chicago and the Grand Central Station Subway renovation, NYC.

RAVE ARCHITEKTEN
Knesebeckstr 13,
D10623 Berlin, Germany
Trained by Bauhaus architects, brothers Jan and Rolf Rave started working together in 1963 shortly after they completed their studies at the TU Berlin and the Ecole des Beaux-Arts in Paris and at the Hochschule fur Bildende Kunste in Berlin respectively. They were joined by Rolf's wife, Roosje Rave in 1990 when Rave Architekten BDA was founded. They frequently take part in design competitions, resulting in 13 projects being awarded 1st prize and subsequently built. They are involved in architecture, interior design and town planning. Notable schemes include terraced housing in Wurttemberg-allee; open plan offices, BfA on Fehrbelliner Platz; the Crematorium in Rugleben; and urban regeneration in Berlin where their housing formed a contrast to the surrounding architecture. They won a

competition for Schoneberger Rathaus a 13-year detailed preservation/restoration scheme on the public areas of this government headquarters in West Berlin. Jan Rave was Chairman of the BDA, Berlin from 1987-93 and in 1994 was the founder and chairman of Fordervereins Architekturpreis Berlin. Rolf Rave has been Professor of Object Design at Fachhochschule in Munster and was Chairman of the advisory council for city design in 1987-9.

DENNIS SANTACHIARA
Alzzaia Naviglio Grande 15
I-20144 Milan, Italy
Dennis Santachiara was born in Reggio-Emilio, Italy, and now lives and works in Milan. He collaborates with major European manufacturers such as Oceano Oltreluce, Artemide, Kartell, Vitra, Yamagiwa, Domodinamica and Zerodisegno. His work has been exhibited in private and public galleries, and he has taken part in the Venice Biennale and Documenta Kassel, as well as the Milan Triennale in 1982, 1984, 1986 and 1988

CHHADA SIEMBIEDA & PARTNERS
400 Oceangate, Suite 1100, Long Beach, CA 90802, USA
Chhada Siembieda & Partners is a design consultancy specialising in hotels and resorts, having completed over 100 projects worldwide. It was originally founded in Hong Kong and opened its California branch in 1982. Completed work includes the original Regent of Hong Kong, the Four Seasons in New York, the Hotel Rafael in Munich and the Hotel Bora Bora in French Polynesia.

SORDO MADALENO Y ASOCIADOS SC
Passeo de la Reforma,
2076-A, 11000 Mexico
Juan Sordo Madaleno Architect set up his own practice in 1937 offering comprehensive services in architecture and interior design. He went into partnership with Javier Sordo Madaleno in 1982. They have worked on a wide range of schemes from private housing, retail outlets, apartment blocks and office buildings to large-scale public buildings, factories and laboratories. Their work has been published internationally and they have collaborated with well know architects in Mexico such as Luis Barragán and Ricardo Legorreta and also abroad with Foster Associates and Skidmore Owens & Merril, Graham & Solano, and Copeland Novak Israel and Simmons.

PHILIPPE STARCK
27 rue Pierre Poli,
92130 Issy-les-Moulineaux,
Paris, France
Philippe Starck was born in Paris in 1949. He worked as a fashion designer for the Pierre Cardin furniture collection, then in the early 1970s he formed his own company making inflatable objects. In the 1980s he designed avant-garde nightclub interiors and he won recognition for his work on Les Bains and La Main Jaune, which were inspired by the science fiction of Philip K. Dick. After a period in New York, he returned to France where he runs his own intentionally small design company Starck Ubik. He has been responsible for major interior design schemes, including François Mitterand's apartment at the Elysée Palace, the Café Costes, and the acclaimed Royalton and Paramount hotels in Manhattan. He has

also created domestic and public multi-purpose buildings such as the headquarters of Asahi Beer in Tokyo. As a product designer he works for companies throughout the world, collaborating with Alessi, Baleri, Baum, Disform, Driade, Flos, Kartell, Rapsel, Up & Up, Vitra, Vuitton and Thomson Consumer Electrics. His many awards include the Grand Prix National de la Création Industrielle. His work can be seen in the collections of the major design museums worldwide. Recent projects include the Delano Hotel in Miami; the Mondrian hotel in Los Angeles; and the Theatron nightclub in Mexico.

ROBERT STERN ARCHITECTS
460 West 34th Street, New York,
NY 10001, USA
Robert Stern Architects was founded in the late 1960s. The practice is involved in architecture, landscape design and interior design, specialising in residential, commercial and institutional work in Europe, Asia and the USA. Its highly distinctive classic revivalism has won numerous prizes, including the National Honor Awards of the American Institute of Architects in 1980, 1985, 1990 and 1991. Recently completed projects include the Norman Rockwell Museum, Stockbridge, Massachusetts; the Newport Bay Hotel, USA; Euro-Disney, Marne-La Vallee, France; the Centre for Jewish Life, Princeton University; the Information Science Building at Stanford University, California; The Walt Disney Feature Animation Building, Burbank, California; the Disney Boardwalk hotel in Miami, and resorts hotels in Japan. Robert Stern graduated from Columbia University in 1960 and from Yale in 1965. Today he is a Professor at the Graduate School of Architecture, Planning and Preservation at Columbia University and has lectured extensively in the USA and abroad. He is the author of several books including 'Modern Classicism' (1988). He serves on the board of directors of the Walt Disney Company, the Chicago Institute of Architecture and Urbanism, and the New York Architectural League. He is currently undertaking two major projects for the Walt Disney Corporation.

WARWICK STONE
c/o Hard Rock Hotel & Casino
Warwick Stone began his career in the 1970s as the rock n' roll costume designer for Freddie Mercury and Manhattan Transfer. In 1982 he landed the job of creative director for Hard Rock America. He is responsible for the interior and exterior design of the hotel and casino, including car sculptures and guitar signage.

STUDIO JAN WICHERS
Mittelweg 162,
20148 Hamburg, Germany
Jan Wichers was born in 1944. Today he has his own studio in Hamburg which employs 10-12 interior architects. As well as interior design his practice is involved with product development and corporate identity for many German and foreign manufacturers of furniture, fabrics, carpets and lighting such as B&B, DePadova, UP&UP, Rosenthal, Villeroy and Boch, Vorwerk and Poltrona Frau. Projects in progress at the moment include shop designs for Gucci, hotels and restaurants in Germany and Spain as well as the Dubai Marine Beach Resort and the Donner-Bank in Hamburg. Jan Wilchers has received national and international

recognition. In 1993 he was awarded the Deutscher Natursteinpreis and his work can be seen in various permanent collections around the world.

STUDIO SOFIELD
380 Lafayette Street, PH No. 2,
New York City 10003, USA
Studio Sofield is a revival of Aero Design which was first established in 1992 by architect William Sofield and interior designer Thomas O'Brian. This practice mixed interior design with a line of custom furniture and decorative accessories upholding the Bauhaus tradition of contemporary design. Today Sofield specialises in residential and garden design as well as all aspects of retail and hospitality. He gained his BA at Princeton University. In 1983 he earned a Helena Rubinstein Fellowship from the Whitney Museum of American Art. Currently he is a Fellow of the Frick Collection and a lecturer at the Parsons School of Design.

SUNWAY DESIGN SDN BHD.
Level 3 Menara SungeiWay,
Jalan Lagun Timur, Bandar,
Sunway, 46150, Petaling Jaya, Malaysia
Sunway Design was founded in 1987 and was formerly known as Design Topics Sdn Bhd. The practice specialises in interior design and decoration, renovation and graphic consultancy for the residential and commercial market. They have acquired expertise in the design of hotels, retail outlets, government departments, showhouses, recreation centres and theme parks as well as residential and condominium projects. Clients include Sunway City Berhad, the SungeiWay Corporation, National Panasonic and Avon Cosmetics.

KENZO TANGE ASSOCIATES,
7-2-21 Akasaka, Minato-ku,
Tokyo, Japan 107
The practice was founded in 1946 as Kenzo Tange Studio becoming known as Kenzo Tange Associates Urbanists and Architects in 1985. Today they have offices in Paris, Singapore and Saudi Arabia. Kenzo Tange became a First Class Licensed Architect in 1952. KTA's international experience covers architecture and urban planning ranging from commercial buildings to entire new cities. They have completed landmark gymnasiums and stadiums worldwide and new capital cities in Abuja, Nigeria, the Federal Twin Capital of Malaysia and the Bandar Seri Begawan in Brunei. Urban planning projects have been undertaken in Japan, China and Europe and city centre designs are nearly complete for Bologna, and Naples. Kenzo Tange has received more than 40 medals from around the world including Gold Medals from the Institute of Architects in Japan, United States, England, France, Germany and Italy. He is also the recipient of the prestigious Commandier dans l'Ordre des Arts et Lettres de France, The Order of Culture in Japan, The Pritzker Architecture Prize of the USA and the Praemium Imperiale of Japan.

ARCHITEKTEN TILLA THEUS UND PARTNER
Bionstr 18, 8006 Zürich,
Switzerland
Tilla Theus was born in 1943 and lives and works in Zürich, Graubunden and Ticino. She studied architecture at the ETH in Zürich, receiving her Diploma in 1969 from Prof. J. Schrader. Subsequently she formed a

partnership with Kurt Rutschmann in 1969, founding her practice Tilla Theus & Partner in 1985.

UNITED DESIGNERS
37 Shad Thames, Butlers Wharf,
London SE1 2NJ.
United Designers is a London-based design consultancy which has quickly progressed from restaurant interiors such as the award-winning Vong to hotel design with the Metropolitan and Clarence hotels. The practice was founded in 1990 under the name of The Hobbesian Trust in collaboration with Sir Terence Conran, working on The Gastrodrome and Quaglino's. Since this time United Designers have continued to create elegant interiors which are designed 'to improve with age'. Projects number the Bobby Jones Bar & Grill on the Vilar do Golf resort in the Algarve and several projects on board 'Celebrity Cruises' luxurious liners.

URBAN DESIGN GROUP INC
1621 Eighteenth Street, Suite 200,
Denver, Colorado 60202, USA
With offices today in Atlanta, Chicago, Denver, Las Vegas and Tulsa, Urban Design Group was founded in 1975 and their work now covers a wide field from complex urban mixed-use development to customized residences. They offer professional services in architecture, urban planning and design, renovation and adaptive re-use, interior and landscape design. They have achieved national and international recognition with numerous design awards and honours from professional organizations. Clients include Amoco, Disney Development Corporation, IBM, Microsoft, Denver Centre Theatre Company and United Artists.

GALERIE WEINAND
Orianplatz 5, D-10999 Berlin,
Germany
The Atelier Weinand provides turnkey services in interior and design projects and specialises in combining economic and ecological considerations. Their clients are mostly hotels, restaurants and shops and at present they are working on the first HempHotel in Germany.

ARCHITEKTURBÜRO ELW, WEITZ AND PARTNER
Bleibtreustrasse 32,
10707 Berlin, Germany
Werner Weitz was originally a partner in the practice, ELW, Eyl, Weitz, Wurmie and Partner but founded his own company in 1995. Projects range from small additions to renovations to new constructions. Notable schemes include the refurbishment and modernisation of the Municipal Authorities in Potsdam, a seminar building and hotel.

BEATA WELLER
Schulstr. 3, 60594 Frankfurt,
Germany
Beate Weller was born in 1956 in Giessen. She studied interior design and after graduating worked for Leptien 3 and Neuheus. Frequent travel to Milan resulted in collaborations with many leading architects and designers as well as contact with Italian manufacturing companies and craftsmen. Since 1992 she has worked independently throughout Europe and in addition to the Art'otels in Potsdam and Dresden, she is responsible for numerous office, retail and other buildings in Oberursel, Frankfurt and Bad Soden.

WHITE ARKITEKTER, AB
Magasinsgatan 10, Box 2502,
Göteborg, Sweden
White Arkitekter is Sweden's largest firm of architectural and planning consultants. It was founded in 1951 and today has several branches within Sweden as well as offices in Brussels and Berlin. They work in nearly every field of architecture, town planning, landscaping and interior design in both the public and private sectors. Although initially they worked primarily within Sweden, today emphasis is placed more and more on overseas schemes and they have been active in Europe, Africa, the middle and Far East and Central America.

WILSON AND ASSOCIATES
3811 Turtle Creek Boulevard,
Suite 1500, Dallas, Texas,
75219 USA
The interior design firm, Wilson and Associates was incorporated in 1978 by Trisha Wilson and his built up an international reputation for the design of hotels, restaurants, clubs and casinos. To date the firm has worked on over 75,000 guest rooms in 150 hotels worldwide and the company now has offices in Dallas, New York, Los Angeles, Singapore and Johannesburg. The designers aim to maintain the style of an area by using local craftsmen, artisans and artists and involve themselves in the custom design of architectural details, furniture, lighting, carpets and fabrics. Wilson and Associates is a seven time winner of the prestigious American Hotel and Motel Association's Gold Key Award for excellence in hotel design.

WIMBERLY ALLISON TONG & GOO
2260 University Drive,
Newport Beach, California, USA
Wimberly Allison Tong & Goo was founded in 1945 and it has become a world-leader in the design of hotels and resorts in over 50 countries with projects throughout the Pacific Rim, Hawaii, across the USA, Mexico, South America, the Caribbean, Europe, Africa and the Middle East. WAT&G projects have been widely acclaimed both by architectural organisations and the international press. The firm has been recognised for its ability to design outstanding facilities which respect the environment and cultural heritage of the location they work in.

YATES-SILVERMAN
4045 South Industrial Road,
Las Vegas, Nevada, NV 89121, USA
The Yates-Silverman practice was founded in 1971 by Charles Silverman and Bill Yates who retired in 1978. It specialises in commercial interior design, particularly for hotels resorts and gaming properties. Silverman graduated from Rutgers University and worked in the family business before moving to California and joining Albert Parvin and Co. Major projects to date include numerous hotels and casinos in Las Vegas and Atlantic City as well as resorts and clubs in New York, New Orleans, Reno, Los Angeles, Palm Springs and Lake Tahoe.

NAME MONDRIAN
ADDRESS 8440 Sunset Boulevard.
Los Angeles. CA 90069. USA
Tel: 212 525 8029
Fax: 212 650 5215
ROOMS/FACILITIES 245 rooms, 'Coco Pazzo' restaurant,
'Skybar', meeting and banqueting
facilities, fitness centre, 24hr
gymnasium
COMPLETION 1996
CLIENT Ian Schrager/Amstar Group Ltd
OPERATOR Ian Schrager/Amstar Group Ltd
ARCHITECT Original building 1959
INTERIOR DESIGNER Philippe Starck
SUBCONTRACTORS/ SUPPLIERS Director of Development:
Michael Overington. Director of
Design: Anda Andrei. Production
Architects: Hank Koning, Tim
Andreas. General Manager: Drew
Schlesinger. Project Manager: Cono
DiZeo. Light Installations: James
Turrell. Video installations: Jean
Baptiste Mondino. Lighting Design:
Arnold Chan, Clark Johnson,
Landscape Consultant: Madison Cox.
Landscape Architect: Laurie Levavi.
Clothing Design: Freddie Leiba

NAME DELANO
ADDRESS 1685 Collins Avenue. Miami Beach,
Florida 33139, USA.
Tel: (0)305 672 2000
Fax: (0)305 532 0099
ROOMS/FACILITIES 238 rooms, Eat in Kitchen. Rose Bar,
8 indoor & outdoor food & beverage
places, 'Water Salon' swimming pool,
gymnasium, movie theatre. meeting
& banqueting facilities
COMPLETION 1995
CLIENT Beach Hotel Associates
OPERATOR Ian Schrager Hotels
ARCHITECT PMG Architects - Peter Gumpel; Jury
Alvarez.
INTERIOR DESIGNER Philippe Starck
SUBCONTRACTORS/ SUPPLIERS General contractor: McDevitt
Sreet Bovis. Lighting: Isometrix.
Landscape architect: Robert Paisley.
Colour consultant: Donald Kaufman
Color. Uniforms: Freddie Leiba.

NAME HOTEL NEW YORK
ADDRESS Kohinginnenhoof No 1, 3072 AD,
Rotterdam, The Netherlands
Tel: (0)10 4390500
Fax: (0)10 4842701
ROOMS/FACILITIES 73 rooms, restaurant and bar seating
400, oyster bar, tea salon, book and
tea shop, barbers
COMPLETION 1993
CLIENT Hotel New York
OPERATOR Independent
ARCHITECT Dorine de Vos
INTERIOR DESIGNER Dorine de Vos
SUBCONTRACTORS/ SUPPLIERS Additional design work: Hans
Loos, Daan van de Have. Uniforms:
Anna van Vliet of Anna & R Kleding.
Imple-mentation and co-design of
cupboards and furniture: Eirk Fateris
ARTISTS L Gus de Ruiter, Klaas Gubbels,
Ondine de Kroo, Luc van Malderen,
Daniel Fauville, Ellen Palsgraaf,
Heddy Gubbels, Leo van der Berg

NAME THE BRUNSWICK HOTEL
ADDRESS 106 Brunswick Street, Glasgow, Great
Britain
Tel: (0)141 552 0001
Fax: (0)141 552 1551

ROOMS/FACILITIES 21 rooms, 2 restaurants, 2
cafés/bars, 1 cocktail bar, limited
conference facilities.
COMPLETION 1995
CLIENT Primavera Leisure
OPERATOR Owner/operator
ARCHITECT Elder & Cannon Architects: Ian
Alexander; Dick Cannon; Tom
Connolly; Bruce Kennedy; John
Russell
INTERIOR DESIGNER Graven Images: Ross Hunter; Jim
Hamilton; Brian Alexander; Janice
Kilpatrick
SUBCONTRACTORS/ SUPPLIERS Main Contractor: Melville
Dundas. Structural Engineers: Blyth
& Blyth Associates. Quantity
Surveyors: Dunne Mitchell & Aikman.
Project Manager: Turner Townsend
Project Management. Façade:
Sterling Stone. Specialist furniture:
Nice House. Shopfitting: Dex
Contracts. Bedside lights: R & S.
Bedroom ceiling lights: Lumino.
General lighting: Litecraft. Light
sculpture: Ewan Hunter

NAME DAS TRIEST
ADDRESS 12 Wiedner Haupstrasse, 1040 Wien,
Austria
Tel: (0)1 589 180
Fax: (0)1 58918 18
ROOMS/FACILITIES 72 rooms, 'Collio' restaurant, 'The
Silver Bar', 2 conference rooms
'Lipizza', 'Piper', flower painted
courtyard
COMPLETION 1995
CLIENT Hof Man Malulan
OPERATOR Hotel Stadt Triest GmbH
ARCHITECT CD Partnership
INTERIOR DESIGNER CD Partnership
SUBCONTRACTORS/ SUPPLIERS Main contractor: Hof Man
Malulan. Lighting: Buro Grommer.
Kitchen: Buro-Stria. Graphics: CD
Partnership. Furniture: Benchmark,
The Conran Shop

NAME THE HEMPEL
ADDRESS Hempel Garden Square,
31/35 Craven Hill Gardens, London
W2 3EA, Great Britain
Tel: (0)171 298 9000
Fax: (0)171 402 4666
ROOMS/FACILITIES 44 bedrooms, 6 apartments, 'Shadow
Bar'. 'I-Thai' restaurant. 4 function
rooms, fitness room, garden square,
video conferencing
COMPLETION 1996
CLIENT Hempel Hotel
OPERATOR Anouska Hempel Management Ltd
ARCHITECT Anouska Hempel
INTERIOR DESIGNER Anouska Hempel

NAME ART'OTEL DRESDEN
ADDRESS Ostra-Allee 33, 01607 Dresden
Germany
Tel: (0)351 357 49220
Fax: (0)351 49 22777
ROOMS/FACILITIES 158 single/doubles, 16 studios,
'Factory', 'Alfredo's' and 'Fish Gallery'
restaurants, 'Factory' bar, 5
conference rooms, fitness facilities,
sauna, boutique, galleries
COMPLETION 1995
CLIENT Gbr Sylvia Gädeke, Gunter Landsberg,
Dirk Gädeke
OPERATOR Art'otel Marketing und
Hotelbetriegesellschaft mbh
ARCHITECT Rolf and Jan Rave

INTERIOR DESIGNER Dennis Santachiara in collaboration
with Kazuyo Komoda and Beate
Weller
SUBCONTRACTORS/ SUPPLIERS Structural engineer: Hippe.
Services engineer: Hagenau. Electrical
services engineer: Eltec KG. Kitchen
planner: Philip Henselmann. Fire
proection consultant: Dr. Schubert.
Project manangement and supervision:
Ruping Consult
ARTWORK A. R. Penck

NAME ART'OTEL POTSDAM
ADDRESS Zeppelinstr. 136,
14471 Potsdam, Germany
Tel: (0)2331 98 15 0
Fax: (0)331 98 15 555
ROOMS/FACILITIES 123 rooms, fish restaurant,
conference facilities, fitness studio
COMPLETION 1995
CLIENT Gruppe Gädeke and Landsberg
OPERATOR Art'otel Marketing und
Hotelbetriegesellschaft mbh
ARCHITECT Architekturbüro Jan & Ralf Rave
INTERIOR DESIGNER Jasper Morrison in cooperation with
AXON and Beate Weller
SUBCONTRACTORS/ SUPPLIERS Atlas table system and handles:
designed by Jasper Morrison.
Furniture suppliers: Cappelini
ARTWORKS Katharina Sieverding,
Frank Oehring

NAME THE METROPOLITAN
ADDRESS 19 Old Park Lane, London
W1Y 4LB, Great Britain
Tel: (0)171 357 6008
Fax: (0)171 357 8008
ROOMS/FACILITIES 155 rooms, conference facilities,
fitness centre, 'Met' bar, 'Nobu'
restaurant
COMPLETION 1997
CLIENT Mr BS Ong and Mrs C Ong
OPERATOR Independent
ARCHITECT Mark Pinney Associates
INTERIOR DESIGNER United Designers: Keith Hobbs; Linzi
Coppick; Alan Hole; Simon Simpson;
Mark Leib; Rachel French; Lorraine
Richer;
SUBCONTRACTORS/ SUPPLIERS Main contractor: Goodman
Hitchins. Subcontractors: Woolston
Electrics; A & B Construction;
Byfords (ceilings); Becher; Ahmarra;
O'Donnell's (joinery); CMC
(metalwork); Smith & Greenwood
(decorators); Light Corporation
(specialist lighting); Norman
Menzies (bathrooms). Soft
furnishings in guest rooms: Sky
Interiors
SPECIALIST CRAFTS Complete fabrications manufactured
the bas relief lobby clock designed
by United Designers. Helen Yardley:
Lobby carpet

NAME THE CLARENCE
ADDRESS 6-8 Wellington Quay, Temple Bar,
Dublin 2, Ireland
Tel: (0)1 670 9000
Fax: (0)1 670 7800
ROOMS/FACILITIES 46 rooms, 3 one and two bedroom
suites, 1 penthouse suite, 'The Tea
room' restaurant, 'The Octagon Bar',
conference and banqueting facilities
for up to 120 people
COMPLETION 1996
CLIENT Harry Crosbie, Bono and The Edge
(U2)
OPERATOR Grace Leo-Andrieu

ARCHITECT	Costello Murray Beaumont: Philip O'Reilly
INTERIOR DESIGNER	United Designers: Keith Hobbs; Linzi Coppick; Simon Simpson; Rachel French
SUBCONTRACTORS/ SUPPLIERS	Main Contractors: MJ Clarke & Sons; O'Donnells (joinery); Breen (electrics). Bedroom furniture & fittings: O'Donnells. Designer Rugs: Helen Yardley. Original Artworks: Gugghi. Graphics: Teresa Riviers. Skylight & Tearoom Window Lighting: Jankowski Lighting. Bedroom tub chairs: Opus. Tearoom chairs & Clarence Chairs: Englender Furniture.

NAME	**ADELPHI HOTEL**
ADDRESS	187 Flinders Lane, Melbourne 3000, Australia
	Tel: (0)3 9650 7555
	Fax: (0)3 9650 2710
ROOMS/FACILITIES	34 rooms, 1 restaurant , 2 bars, conference facilities, leisure complex, 25m rooftop swimming pool
COMPLETION	1993
CLIENT	Adelphi Pty Ltd
OPERATOR	Independent
ARCHITECT	Denton Corker Marshall Pty Ltd
INTERIOR DESIGNER	Denton Corker Marshall Pty Ltd
SUBCONTRACTORS/ SUPPLIERS	Main Contractor: Cotneco Pty Ltd. Structural consultant: Ove Arup & Partners. Mechanical and Electrical consultants: Lincolne Scott. Furniture: Denton Corker Marshall Pty Ltd. Lights: Denton Corker Marshall Pty Ltd. Floor Rugs: Rugs by Design; Ammolite Pty

NAME	**THE POINT HOTEL**
ADDRESS	34 Bread Street, Edinburgh EH3 9AF
	Tel: (0)131 221 9919
	Fax: (0)131 221 9929
ROOMS/FACILITIES	130 rooms including 5 suites, 2 meeting rooms. Restaurant. Café Bar; Fitness Centre with Sauna, car parking, landscaped courtyard
COMPLETION	1995-7
CLIENT	Kantel
OPERATOR	Kantel
ARCHITECT	Andrew Doolan Architects
INTERIOR DESIGNER	Andrew Doolan Architects
SUBCONTRACTORS/ SUPPLIERS	Construction: Kantel. Colin Reynolds & Associates; Brennan Associates; Enconsult; Iain Abbot, Broughton Building; WBM Plumbing; David Thomson Electrical Services; Ian Clyde Builders; RCD Decorators; Capital Stone; Nancy Downs Interiors; Justice Furniture; Inhouse Contracts; Tony Walker Interiors; A B Mearns; A Jack Glaziers; Safety First Films; Floor Coverings International
ARTISTS	Hock Aun Teh, Caroline McNairn, Fionna Carlisle, Lucy Ross, Beckerman Balken

NAME	**BLEIBTREU HOTEL BERLIN**
ADDRESS	Bleibtreustrasse 31, D-10707 Berlin, Germany
	Tel: (0)30 884 740
	Fax: (0)30 884 74 444
ROOMS/FACILITIES	60 rooms, Bleibtreu '31' restaurant, 'Blue Bar' espresso bar, steam baths, flower and book shops
COMPLETION	1995

CLIENT	Galerie Weinand
OPERATOR	Savoy
ARCHITECT	Werner Weitz
INTERIOR DESIGNER	Atelier Weinand
SUBCONTRACTORS/ SUPPLIERS	Terrazzo work: Concreta. Mosaic glaze in bathroom and tiles: Villeroy and Boch. Room furniture: Porro Industria Mobili. Sofas and armchairs: Colber. Light fittings: Brendel.
ARTISTS	Herbert Jacob Weinand, Stefen Zwicky, Renate von Brevern, Bonomo Faita, Rosmarie Sansonetti, Jose Vermeesch, Hanna Frenzel, Katja Hajek, Anne Jud

NAME	**HOTEL LA PÉROUSE**
ADDRESS	Cours des 50 Otages, 3 Allée Duquesne, 44000 Nantes, France
	Tel: (0)2 40 89 75 00
	Fax: (0)2 40 89 76 00
ROOMS/FACILITIES	47 rooms with air conditioning, soundproofing, direct telephone, Canal and satellite channels
COMPLETION	1993
CLIENT	Sarl La Pérouse
ARCHITECT	Barto + Barto
INTERIOR DESIGNER	Barto + Barto
SUBCONTRACTORS/ SUPPLIERS	Main contractor: Entreprise Bonnier. Coordinating Architect: Pierrie Mazeron. Façade and stone roof: Rocamat France. Stone detailing: Entreprise Pernes. Exterior woodwork: Atlantic Ouvertures. Hall daybed: Day Bed Eileen Grey, IDM. Bedroom chairs: Zig Zag Rietvield, IDM. Breakfast room chairs: Hamlet Machine - Wilson. Breakfast room lighting: Condor - Loreley.

NAME	**ROGNER-BAD BLUMAU**
ADDRESS	Rogner-Bad Blumau, A-82838 Blumau 100, Austria
	Tel: (0)3383 51000
	Fax: (0)3383 5100802
ROOMS/FACILITIES	247 double rooms, 24 apartments, 3 restaurants, coffee house, bar, conference and function rooms for up to 200 people, in and outdoor swimming pools with fresh and thermal waters, sauna facilities, Roman and Turkish baths, jacuzzi, herb room, health and wellness centre, beauty salon, leisure and sport facilities.
COMPLETION	1997
CLIENT	Rogner International Hotels & Resorts GesmbH
OPERATOR	Rogner International Hotels & Resorts GesmbH
ARCHITECT	Peter Pelikan
INTERIOR DESIGNER	Rogner Austria, Mrs Melitta Rogner, Mr Franz Ulbing
SUBCONTRACTORS/ SUPPLIERS	Project Control: Immorebt AG. Civil Engineer: Alchholzer. Specialist civil engineer: Bauer GmbH. Lighting and ventilation systems: Almos. Golf Course: Austrogolf GmbH. Furniture: Ehrenhofler GmbH. Nursey/kindergarten fittings: Eibe. Wooden Windows and Furniture: KAPO GembH. Treatment rooms and facilities: Klmox Hubner. Ceramics, tiles and sanitary equipment: Koll Ceramik GmbH. Rooms and internal fittings: Spiel Dach Glas GmbH.
ARTIST	Friedensreich Hundertwasser

NAME	**SEIDLER HOTEL PELIKAN**
ADDRESS	Podbielskistrasse 145, 30177 Hanover, Germany
	Tel: (0)511 90 930
	Fax: (0)511 90 93 555
ROOMS/FACILITIES	138 rooms, international restaurant, Japanese restaurant, Harry's New York Bar, conference facilities for 5-250 people, health spa with swimming pool
COMPLETION	1995
CLIENT	Simon Grundbesitz Verwaltungs KG
OPERATOR	Seidler Hotel Pelikan GmbH & Co Betriebsgesellschaft
ARCHITECT	Dieter Neikes. Project Manager: Stephan Guder. Team: Egon Cremer, Claudia Hilgers, Enrique Ortega, Kurt Leopold, Gabriele Knapp, Doris Vogelsang
INTERIOR DESIGNER	Aut Design, Harald Klein
SUBCONTRACTORS/ SUPPLIERS	Furniture: Andreu World, Baler. Giorgetti, Montina, Moroso. Lighting: Kreon-Leuchten

NAME	**SHERATON HOTEL**
ADDRESS	Aérogare Charles de Gaulle 2, BP 30051-95716 Roissy, France
ROOMS/FACILITIES	242 rooms, 14 suites, 'Les Etoiles' restaurant, 'Les Saisons' restaurant, 'Galaxie' bar, fitness centre, 24hr business centre, 6 meeting rooms
COMPLETION	1996
CLIENT	ITT Sheraton
OPERATOR	ITT Sheraton
ARCHITECT	Martinet Architecture
INTERIOR DESIGNER	Ecart
SUBCONTRACTORS/ SUPPLIERS	Design of interchange module: TGV/RER Stations. Builder: CBC Heulin Construction. Consultants: Impedance SA (acoustics); Aartill (lighting); Restauration Conseil (kitchens). Room layout: Chantiers Baudet SA. 5.20 level layouts: Lambro Contact Ltd. Decorative metalwork and light fittings: LCSD. Room furniture: Durlat. 5.20 level furniture: Laval. Business armchairs: Ecart International

NAME	**RADISSON MORIAH PLAZA HOTEL**
ADDRESS	155 Hayarkon Street, Tel Aviv 63453, Israel
	Tel: (0)3 5216666
	Fax: (0)3 5271065
ROOMS/FACILITIES	357 rooms, 'Cna'an' restaurant, 'Yarden' restaurant, lobby lounge and bar, 5 banqueting halls, swimming pool, jewellery store, newsstand, souvenir shop, beauty parlour, fitness club
COMPLETION	1996
CLIENT	Radisson Hotels
OPERATOR	Radisson Hotels Worldwide
ARCHITECT	Ilan Pivko
INTERIOR DESIGNER	Colin Gold
SUBCONTRACTORS/ SUPPLIERS	Main Contractor: Epstein & Co. Furniture: Kastiel Ltd. Chandeleirs and specialist furniture: Colin Gold, Ilan Pivko. Shop fitting: Ephraim Badian Ltd. General lighting: Kamchi Ltd.

NAME	**FUKUOKA HYATT REGENCY HOTEL**
ADDRESS	MKD - 7 Sphinx Centre, Fukuoka, Japan
	Tel: (0)33 265 5551
	Fax: (0)33 261 6504

ROOMS/FACILITIES 260 rooms, business centre; restaurant; bar; banquet hall; retail facilities; café
COMPLETION 1993
CLIENT Fukuoka Jisho Co. Ltd
OPERATOR Hyatt International
ARCHITECT Michael Graves Architects - Michael Graves, Thomas Rowe, Patrick Mulberry, Alexey Grigorieff, Kim Armour, Wendy Bradford, Jesse Castaneda, Lorissa Kimm, Andrea Wang
INTERIOR DESIGNER Michael Graves Architects
SUBCONTRACTORS/ SUPPLIERS Associate architect: Fukuoka Jisho Company. Main Contractor: Maeda Corporation. Exterior masonry/cladding: ADVAN. Pre-patinated copper cladding: Tateyama Alumininum; Sankyo Alumninium. Lighting: custom designed by Michael Graves. Cabinetwork & custom woodwork: Mitsukoshi. Gold leaf: Sumitomo 3M. Fixed seating chairs & tables: MGA

NAME LINGOTTO MÉRIDIEN
ADDRESS Via Nizza 262, Torino, Italy
Tel: (0)11 664 2000
Fax: (0)11 664 2001
ROOMS/FACILITIES 244 rooms, 2 junior suites, 12 suites, 'La Rivoli' restaurant, 'Garden' bar, 2 meeting halls seating 80 people
COMPLETION 1995
CLIENT Lingotto and Hotel Méridien
OPERATOR Lingotto and Hotel Méridien
ARCHITECT Renzo Piano Building Workshop
INTERIOR DESIGNER Franco Mirenzi (Unimark)
SUBCONTRACTORS/ SUPPLIERS Main Contractor: Associazione Temporanea d'Impresse. Consultants: Ove Arup and Partners (structural and mechanical engineering); A. I. Engineering; Fiat Engineering. Steel structure, glazing system and fittings in the bubble: Gruppo Bodino. Insulated glass (bubble): Hardglass. Lighting (bubble): i Guzzini. Lighting: P. Castiglioni. Graphics: P. L. Cerri, Ecco SpA. Interiors: F. Santolini. Director of works: Studio Vitone e Associati (to 1992); F. Levi; G. Mottino (second phase). Furniture supplier: A Studio Srl.; Serioli Arredamenti' Bonacina

NAME SOHO GRAND HOTEL
ADDRESS 310 West Broadway At Grand Street, New York, NY 10013, USA
Tel: (0)212 334 4077
Fax: (0)212 334 7597
ROOMS/FACILITIES 369 rooms, 4 penthouse suites, grand bar, bistro, lobby lounge, restaurant, fitness room, business facilities
COMPLETION 1996
CLIENT Hartz Mountain Industries
OPERATOR Independent
ARCHITECT Helpern Architects: David Paul Helpern (Principal in charge); Catherine Mikic (Project Designer); Barry Yanku (Project Architect); Richard Rose (Project Manager)
INTERIOR DESIGNER William Sofield
SUBCONTRACTORS/ SUPPLIERS Main Contractors: RC Dolner Inc (General Contractor). Main Suppliers & Consultants: Architectural Building Associate. Lighting Consultants: Johnson Schwinghammer. Lobby fitting suppliers: Aero, Beverley Furniture Manufacturing Company,

Studio Sofield, Chris Lehrecke Furniture (furniture), Aero (lamps). Canal House fitting suppliers: Artumus (lighting); Historical Materialism (lamp); Urban Archaeology (Maitre d' stand, wine storage cabinet, antique jewellery case). Room fittings suppliers: Studio Sofield (furniture); Aero (lighting);
ARTISTS Joseph Stashkevetch 'Trestle No. 23' (1996), lobby

NAME HOTEL KYOCERA
ADDRESS 1409-01 Mitsugi, Hayato-cho, Aira-gun, Kagoshima 899-51, Japan
Tel: (0)995-43-7111
Fax: (0)995-43-7331
ROOMS/FACILITIES 183 rooms, 4 restaurants, lounge bar, 3 banqueting halls one accommodating 550 people, health spa with swimming pool and natural hot spring, Japanese and Christian wedding chapels
COMPLETION 1995
CLIENT Kyocera Development Company
OPERATOR Ryuji Nagata, Hotel Kyocera
ARCHITECT Kisho Kurokawa Architects and Associates
INTERIOR DESIGNER Kisho Kurokawa Architects and Associates
SUBCONTRACTORS/ SUPPLIERS Main Contractor: Taisei Corporation
ARTISTS Junji Yoshii (paintings); Shinya Nakamura (sculptures); Yoko Yamamoto (prints in the bar)

NAME BLÅ HALLEN
ADDRESS Eriksberg, Maskingatan 5, S-417 16 Göteborg, Sweden
ROOMS/FACILITIES 133 rooms; restaurant, theatre; bar; conference rooms; offices; shops; garage.
COMPLETION 1962, rebuilt 1990-93
CLIENT HB Blå Hallen
OPERATOR Independent
ARCHITECT White arkitekter AB. Project planning adminstration: Stig Olsson. Project team: Bengt Berglund; Ingemar Borjesson; Brigetta Illes; Dan Larsson; Bo Svensson; Maria Ohman
INTERIOR DESIGNER White arkitekter
SUBCONTRACTORS/ SUPPLIERS Interior design of dining room, Bar 67 and conference room: Margareta and Rolf Åberg, interior design architects (SIR). Design of hotel bedrooms: AB Gunnar Svensson. Building contractor: Skanska Vast AB. Structural engineering: VBK. Konsulterande ingenjorer. Project adminstration: J & W Bygg & Anlaggning. Public area furniture: Jonas Bohlin, John Kandell, Mats Theselius, Kallemo. Reception and lobby furniture: Friis and Molthe manufactured by Randers. Consultant landscape architect: Bruno Richter
ARTISTS Leif Ericson, Gorel Steg, Ulf Trotzig, Olle Zetterquist

NAME HOTEL MARTINSPARK GMBH & CO.
ADDRESS Mozartstrasse 2. A- 6850 Dornbirn, Austria
Tel: (0)5572 3760
Fax: (0)5572 3760 376

ROOMS/FACILITIES 88 rooms, 12 apartments, restaurant, bar, 4 conference rooms seating 200, sauna, solarium
COMPLETION 1994, conference facilities 1996
CLIENT I + R Schertler Gmbh
OPERATOR Vienna International
ARCHITECT Baumschlager Eberle Architekturbüro
INTERIOR DESIGNER Baumschlager Eberle Architekturbüro
SUBCONTRACTORS/ SUPPLIERS Main Contractor: I + R Schertler. Project Manager: Baumeister Fink. Structural designer: Rusch und Diem
ARTISTS Flatz, Moholy-Nagy, Imi Knobel, Ingmar Algae, Eduard Heube

NAME KEMPINSKI AIRPORT HOTEL
ADDRESS Airport München Terminalstrasse Mitte 20, 85356 München Germany
Tel: (0)89 97 82 35 14
Fax:(0)89 21 25 20 00
ROOMS/FACILITIES 343 standard rooms; 46 suites, beer garden; banquet hall; conference rooms; 'Charles Lindbergh' restaurant, 'Spirit of St. Louis' restaurant and bar, 'Atrium' bar, espresso bar, bistro, swimming pool, and fitness centre; business centre
COMPLETION 1994
CLIENT Flughafen München Gmbh
OPERATOR Kempinski Hotels
ARCHITECT Murphy/Jahn: Helmut Jahn; Sam Scaccia; Rainer Schildknecht; Steven Cook; Steven Niles; Lothar Paschar; Antonio A. Pelipada; John Myefski; Richard Ehlert
INTERIOR DESIGNER Studio Wichers
SUBCONTRACTORS/ SUPPLIERS Main Contractor: Hinteregger/Heinemann, Gartner/Fischer. Structural Engineer (steel): Schlaich, Bergermann und Partner. Structural Engineer (concrete): Cronauer Beratung und Planung. Mechanical Engineers: Cronauer Beratung und Planung; Kuehn Lehr Associates; Landscape Architect: Peter Walker, William Johnson & Partners, Prof. Rainer Schmidt. Landscape Contractor: May Landschaftsbau GmbH & Co. Lighting: Francis Krahe & Associates

NAME HOTEL ZÜRICHBERG
ADDRESS 710 Hotel Zürichberg Orellistrasse 21, 8044 Zürich, Switzerland.
Tel & Fax: (0)268 35 35
ROOMS/FACILITIES 67 rooms, Kiebitz' restaurant, 'Colibri' coffee bar, 4 conference rooms, history kursaal for meetings and conferences
COMPLETION 1994-5
CLIENT Zürcher Frauen Verein
OPERATOR Owner/manager
ARCHITECT Marianne Burkhalter and Christian Sumi with Toni Wirth, Giorgio Bello, Marc v Gilbert
INTERIOR DESIGNER Marianne Burkhalter and Christian Sumi
SUBCONTRACTORS/ SUPPLIERS Project management: Arthur Schlatter, Rolf Schudel. Landscape architects: Kienast Vogt Partner. Engineer: J. Spahn. Building contractor: Locher & cie AG. Metal/steel construction: Ita Sohne GmbH; Schreinerarbeiten Brack & Co.; Muller Schreinerei

NAME HOTEL WIDDER
ADDRESS Ennweg 7, CH-8001 Zürich,
Switzerland.
Tel: (0)1 224 25 26
Fax: (0)1 224 24 24
ROOMS/FACILITIES 42 rooms, 7 suites, 'Turmsubli'
restaurant, 'Wirtschaft zur Schtund'
bar, banqueting facilities for up to
200 people, garden, library, garage
COMPLETION 1995
CLIENT UBS Schweizerische Baukgesellschaft
OPERATOR Widder Hotel AG
ARCHITECT Tilla Theus und Partner AG
INTERIOR DESIGNER Tilla Theus und Partner AG
SUBCONTRACTORS/ Main contractor: Karl Steiner
SUPPLIERS Generalunternehmung AG

NAME HOTEL REY JUAN CARLOS
ADDRESS Arda Diagonal 661-671, Barcelona,
Spain
Tel: (0)3 448 0808
Fax: (0)3 448 0607
ROOMS/FACILITIES 325 rooms, 2 Royal suites, 1
Presidential suite, 34 suites, 3
restaurants, 2 bars, retail outlets,
parking, 2 swimming pools, terraces,
tennis courts health club, pitt and
putt golf green
COMPLETION 1993 - fitness centre 1996
CLIENT Barcelona Projects SA
OPERATOR Barcelona Projects/Conrad
International
ARCHITECT Joseph Cartana and Carlos Ferrater,
Alberto de Salas (chief architect),
Antonio Casaus, Alberto Malavia,
Pedro Vaquer, Agustin Molina
(Hotel); Joan Boada, Jordi Roma,
Joan Soldevilla, Lluis Dieguez
(fitness centre)
INTERIOR DESIGNER Cartana and Ferrater (public spaces);
Amykassa SA, bars and restaurants
Briales del Amo arqs. (fitness centre)
SUBCONTRACTORS/ Contractor: Agroman.
SUPPLIERS Collaborators: Antonio Casaus arq,
Alberto Malavia, Pedro Vaquer, Agustin
Molina. Elena Mateu arq (fitness
centre). Design of rooms, bars and
restaurants: Amykasa SA. Scenery and
furniture: Amykasa. Mechanical
installations: Injar SA. Interior
marble: Macsa. Exterior Marble:
Firmasa. Glasswork: La Veneciana

NAME WESTIN REGINA
LOS CABOS HOTEL
ADDRESS Carretera Trasnpeninsular KM. 22,
San Jose Del Carbo,
Baja California Sur, Mexico,
PO Box 145, CP 23400.
Tel: (0)114 290 01
Fax: (0)114 290 10
ROOMS/FACILITIES 305 rooms including 39 suites, 12
junior suites and 63 villas, 'La
Cascada' restaurant, 'Arrecifes'
restaurant, 'El set' restaurant' 'La
Playa' restaurant, La 'Cantina' sports
bar, conference facilities for 900;
fitness club, health spa, 5 outdoor
swimming pools, 2 indoor swimming
pools, golf courses, retail outlets
COMPLETION 1993
CLIENT Bancomer SA
OPERATOR Westin Hotels and Resorts
ARCHITECT Sordo Madaleno y Asociados SC -
Javier Sordo Madaleno, Jose de
Yturbe Bernal (design concept);
Humberto Mendoza (project
direction); Armando Zarraga
(architectural supervision)

INTERIOR DESIGNER Division y Diseno de Interiores
SUBCONTRACTORS/ Structural contractor Alejandro
SUPPLIERS Fierro. Electrical Contractor: Arellano
Ingenieria. Hydrological Contractor:
Gutierrez Tello y Asociados.
Construction: Ingenieros Civiles
Asoicaiados (ICA). Architectural
supervision and Landscape
Architecture: Sordo Madalano y
Asociados. Construction
Coordinator: Rual

NAME SEA HAWK HOTEL & RESORT
ADDRESS Fukuoka City, Japan
Tel: (0)92 844 7777
Fax: (0)92 847 1602
ROOMS/FACILITIES 1,052 rooms, continental and japanese
resaurants, bar, brasserie, café, library,
retail outlets, banqueting halls,
conference facilities, convention hall,
wedding chapel and halls, photo
studio, Soto Koto Health Club with
indoor and outdoor swimming pools
COMPLETION 1995
CLIENT Fukuoka Daiei Real Estate Inc
OPERATOR Hyatt International
ARCHITECT Cesar Pelli & Associates: Cesar Pelli
(Design Principal). Fred W. Clarke
(Project Principal). Design Team
Leaders: Rafael Pelli; William Butler.
Project Director: Jun Mitsui.
Designers: Bruce Davis; David
Chen; David Johbnson; Steven
Marcetti,; Mihaly Turbcz; Roberta
Weinberg; Takahiro Sato; Hiroyuki
Takahara
INTERIOR DESIGNER Cesar Pelli & Associates/ Takenaka
Corporation
SUBCONTRACTORS/ General Contractor: Joint
SUPPLIERS Venture: Takenaka Corporation;
Maeda Corporation; Ichiken Co.
Ltd. Landscape Design: Balmori
Associates Inc. Architectural
Lighting Design Consultant:
Cline Bettridge, Bernstein Lighting
Design Inc. Architectural Lighting:
Matsushita Electric Works,
Ltd. Engineers: Takenaka
Corporation

NAME HOTEL OCEAN 45
SEAGAIA PHOENIX RESORT
ADDRESS Miyazaki, Japan
Tel: (0)985 21 1133
Fax: (0)985 21 1144
ROOMS/FACILITIES 753 rooms, seven western style
restaurants, three Japanese restaurants;
one Chinese restaurant, seven bar
lounges, three meeting rooms,
athletic club and lounge,
swimmimg pool
COMPLETION 1994
CLIENT Phoenix Resort Co. Ltd
OPERATOR Phoenix Resort Co. Ltd
ARCHITECT Y. Ashihara Architect and Assoc.
INTERIOR DESIGNER Y. Ashihara Architect and Assoc; Design
Division of Shimizu Corporation
SUBCONTRACTORS/ Construction: Shimizu
SUPPLIERS Corporation. Air conditioning: Takasago
Netsugaku. Electrical Work: Kyudenko.
Contractors: Shimizu Corporation,
Nissan Construction; Kumagai Gumi;
Mitsui Construction; JDC; Matsuo
Construction; Sakashita Gumi; Sida
Gumi; Taisei Corporation; Mitsubishi
Heavy Industries; Yoshihara
Construction; Kajima Corporation;
Obayashi Corporation

NAME NEW YORK, NEW YORK
ADDRESS 3790 Las Vegas Blv Sou, Las Vegas
NV 89109, USA
Tel: (0)1 800 740 6969
Fax: (0)1 800 740 6920
ROOMS/FACILITIES 2,033 rooms; 6 restaurants; 7 bars;
2 lounges; 3 meeting rooms; health
& fitness spa with outdoor pool, 9
retail outlets; Manahatten Express
roller coaster; Coney Island
Emporium, 1,000 seat theatre,
casino, nightclubs, wedding chapel
COMPLETION 1997
CLIENT New York, New York Partners Inc
OPERATOR MGM Grand Inc. and Primadonna
Resorts Inc
ARCHITECT Gaskin & Bezanski Architecture and
Engineering
INTERIOR DESIGNER Yates Silverman Inc: Joyce E.
Roians; AIA; Project Design Director.
Public Space Designer: Robyn
MacAdams, Suite & Guestroom
Interior Designer: Shirley Ho, Senior
Design Consultant
SUBCONTRACTORS/ General Contractor: Marnell
SUPPLIERS Corrao & Associates

NAME HARD ROCK HOTEL
ADDRESS 4455 Paradise Road, Las Vegas NV
89109, USA
Tel: (0)702 693 5000
Fax: (0)702 693 5010
ROOMS/FACILITIES 340 rooms (28 suites); casino, 2
restaurants, retail store, sundry
shop, video arcade, ticket desk,
beach club, athletic club, arena,
175ft swimming pool, rock
memorabilia collection
COMPLETION 1995
CLIENT Peter A. Morton
OPERATOR Hard Rock International
ARCHITECT Franklin D. Israel Design Associates
INTERIOR DESIGNER Aero Studios (bedrooms); Sophie
Harvey Design Studios (restaurant),
Howard Fields (pool and landscape);
Hard Rock Design Staff (casino)
SUBCONTRACTORS/ Main Contractor: Perini -
SUPPLIERS Construction Company Headquarters.
Hotel Design Consultant: Warwick
Stone. Millwork: Quality Cabinet.
Neon Signs: Young Electric Sign
Company. Games tables: Paulson
Dice Company. Main Suppliers: John
Greenburg Retails Store

NAME SUNWAY LAGOON
ADDRESS 1 Jalan PJS 11/15, Bandar Sunway,
PO Box 3082, Pusat Mel Subang Jaya
USJ, 47590 Petaling Jaya, Malaysia
Tel: (0)582 8000
Fax: (0)582 8001
ROOMS/FACILITIES 439 rooms, ballroom for 2,300
people, swimming pool, restaurants,
kindergarten, health club,
conference facilities, disco, piano
lounge, business centre, car parking.
Connected by monorail and walkway
to the Sunway Lagoon Theme Park
and Shopping Mall
COMPLETION 1997
CLIENT Sunway Resort Hotel
OPERATOR Allson International Hotel & Resorts
ARCHITECT Akitek Akiprima
INTERIOR DESIGNER Sunway Design
SUBCONTRACTORS/ Main contractor: Sungei Way
SUPPLIERS Construction Berhard. Direct
contractor (swimming pool, deck,
kiddie camo, health centre,
auditorium): PRK Builders. Structural

Engineer: Wong Boon Chong Jurutera Perunding. M & E Engineer: Zainudddin Parsons & Brinckerhoff (M) Sdn Bhd. Lighting consultant: Lighting Point. Furniture supplier: Chung Kwok Furniture; TPO PTE Ltd; Hometrend. Soft furniture suppliers: Interior selection. Artifacts and light fittings supplier: Lightstyle

NAME THE PALACE OF THE LOST CITY
ADDRESS Sun City Boputhatswana
Tel: (0)14 6521000
Fax: (0)14 6573111
ROOMS/FACILITIES 328 rooms, including suites, 'Crystal Court' restaurant, 'Villa Del Palazzo' restaurant, 18 hole championship golf course, water park with wave pool, pool terrace, 'Tusk' lounge and bar
COMPLETION 1993
CLIENT Sun International, Ltd
OPERATOR Sun International Hotels and Resorts
ARCHITECT Wimberly Allison Tong & Goo Inc (California Office): Gearld L. Allison; Eduard Aguilar Robles; Bobby L Caragay
INTERIOR DESIGNER Wilson & Associates (Texas): Trisha Wilson; James Carry; Randall Huggins
SUBCONTRACTORS/ SUPPLIERS Associated Architects: Burg Doherty Bryant & Partners, MV3 Architects. Civil Engineers: Kampel Ambramowitz Yawitch & Partners. Mechanical Engineers: Watson Edwards Inc. Landscape Architects: Top-Turf & Associates. Stone facings: Rock & Waterscape Systems, Inc. Water Feature Consultant: Aquatic Design Group. Landscape Lighting: John Watson Landscape Illumination. Architectural Precast Sculptor: Art, Sculpture & Production, Joe Wertheimer. Project Manager: Schneid Israelite & Partners

NAME WILDERNESS LODGE
ADDRESS 901 Timberline Road, Lake Buena Vista, Florida 32530-100, USA
Tel: 407 824 3200
Fax: 407 824 3232
ROOMS/FACILITIES 728 rooms, 29 suites, 'Whispering Canyon' café, 'Artist Point' restaurant, swimming pool, children's pool, hot tub, erupting geyser
COMPLETION 1994
CLIENT Disney Development Corporation
OPERATOR Disney Development Corporation
ARCHITECT Urban Design Group, Peter H. Dominick Jr., Ronald D. Armstrong, Randal Johnson
INTERIOR DESIGNER Wilson & Associates, Susan Seifert, Michelle Merdith, Roger Harris, Larry Wainwright
SUBCONTRACTORS/ SUPPLIERS Main Contractor: Centex Rooney Construction Company Inc. Structural Engineer: O. E. Olsen & Assoc. Mechanical and electrical engineer: ABS Consultants. Civil Engineer: Ivey Harris and Walls. Landscape Architect: Roy Ashley & Assoc. Acoustics: Merrick & Co. Fireplace Design: Robert Reid. Fireplace screen: Tim Burrows and Jay Wood. Totem poles: Dwayne Pasco. Lighting: Lighting Design Alliance. Graphics: Communications arts, Inc. Furniture: Adele Kerr, Stickley , Carmen Massoud, Nicholas James. Rugs: Allegro. Lighting: Arroyo. Chandeliers:

T.A. Greene. Log railings: Oregon Log Holmes. Bronze figues and column carving: William Robertson
ARTISTS Albert Biscrstadt, Thomas Moran, Thomas Hill, Parker Blake Inc.

NAME DISNEY BOARDWALK
ADDRESS Lake Buena Vista, Florida, 3283 CA, USA
Tel: (0)818 567 5571
Fax: (0)818 566 9870
ROOMS/FACILITIES 378 rooms including 16 suites, business centre, 'Muscles and Bustles' Health club, 'Little Toot's Children's Activity Centre restaurants, bars, retail outlets, outdoor swimming pool, miniature golf course, arcades
COMPLETION 1996
CLIENT Disney Development Company
OPERATOR Walt Disney World/Resort Development
ARCHITECT Design Architect: Robert A.M. Stern Architects: Paul Whale; John Gilmer; John Saunders; Janyne Whitford; Paul Zamek;
INTERIOR DESIGNER Design One: Principal in Charge: Sue Firestone; Senior Designer: Kirk Nix, Designer: Rebecca Holt
SUBCONTRACTORS/ SUPPLIERS Architect of Record: HKS. Project Manager: Paul Katen. Project Coordinator: Todd Lenahan; DVC Construction. Development Manager. Landscape Architect: EDAW Inc. Graphic Designer: RTKL Associates Inc. Structural Engineer: Brockette Davis Drake. Structural Engineer (Peer review): O. E. Olsen and Associates Inc. Civil Engineer: Ivey Harris and Walls Inc. MEP: W.L. Thompson Consulting Engineers. MEP Engineer (Peer review): Carter and Burgess Inc. Acoustic Engineer: Cerami and Associates, Inc. Vertical Transportation Consultant: Persohn Hahn and Associates. Special Systems Consultant: Architectural and Facilities Engineering; Vista-United Communications. Accessibility Consultant: Universal Designers and Consultants Inc. Moisture Protection Consultant: CH2MHill. Lighting Design Consultant: Lighting Design Alliance. Pool Consultant: Evans and Hammond Inc. Roof Consultant: Cox Assoc., Inc.

NAME SHUTTERS ON THE BEACH
ADDRESS 1 Pico Boulevard, Santa Monica, California, USA 90405
Tel: (0)31 0 458 0030
Fax: (0)310 587 1741
ROOMS/FACILITIES 198 rooms, 'Pedals' restaurant, 'One Pico' restaurant, lounge, 'Handlebar' bar with live music, outside swimming pool, fitness centre, sauna
COMPLETION 1993
CLIENT E.T. Whitehall Santa Monica Partners LP
OPERATOR The Edward Thomas Hospitality Corporation
ARCHITECT Hill Glazier Architects Project Team John C. Hill, Robert C. Glazier
INTERIOR DESIGNER Hill Glazier Architects; Paul Draper and Associates (restaurant and bar)
SUBCONTRACTORS/ SUPPLIERS General contractor: Perini Building Co. Structural Engineer: Peter Cullye & Accociates. Mechanical Engineer: Interface Engineering. Electrical Engineer: Toft Wolff Farrow Associates. Landscape Architects: Smith & Smith. Lighting Consultants: Craig Roberts Associates

NAME POUSADA SANTA MARIA DE FLOR DE ROSA
ADDRESS 7430 Crato, Portugal
Tel (0)45 99 72 10
Fax: (0)45 99 72 12
ROOMS/FACILITIES 24 rooms (17 with terrace), restaurant seating 110, banqueting hall for 110, bar, outdoor swimming pool, golf course, hunting facilities
COMPLETION 1995
CLIENT Enatur - Pousadas de Portugal SA
OPERATOR Pousadas
ARCHITECT Joao Luís Carrilho da Graça, Ines Lobo, Anne Demoustier, Pedro Domingos, Nuno Matos, Favio Barbini, Joao Trindade, Maria Joao Silva, Luis Goncalves
INTERIOR DESIGNER Joan Luís Carrilho da Graça
SUBCONTRACTORS/ SUPPLIERS Structure: STA Segadaes Tavares. Electrical Installations: Eng/Ruben Sobral. HVAC: Eng. Jose Galvao Teles

NAME REGENT RESORT CHIANG MAI
ADDRESS Mae Rim-Samoeng Old Road, Mae Rim, Chiang Mai 50180, Thailand
Tel: (0)53 298 181
Fax: (0)53 298 189
ROOMS/FACILITIES 64 pavilion suites, eight residences, 'Sala Mae Rim' restaurant, 'Elephant' bar, pool terrace and bar, swimming pool, health club, beauty salon, business function pavilion
COMPLETION 1995
CLIENT Regent International
OPERATOR Regent Hotels and Peter Burwash
ARCHITECT Chulathat Kitbutr
INTERIOR DESIGNER John Lightbody Abacus
SUBCONTRACTORS/ SUPPLIERS Architectural collaborator: Leg Bunnag Architects. Main contractor: West Con Co., Ltd. Project Manager: Project Asia. Building services Engineer: Loxley (Thailand) Co. Lighting: Project Lighting Company. Kitchen Design: Allied Metals. Landscape: Bensley Design Group

NAME KINGFISHER BAY
ADDRESS Fraser Island
Tel: (0)71 203 333
Fax: (0)71 279 333
ROOMS/FACILITIES 152 hotel rooms; 110 self contained villas; 'Mahano'; 'Seabelle' restaurants; 4 bars; conference facilities; 4 pools, watersports, general store; beauty salon; bakery; child care; eco tours
COMPLETION 1992
CLIENT Kingfisher Bay Resorts Village Pty Ltd.
OPERATOR Tourism Leisure Corporation
ARCHITECT Guymer Bailey Architects: Tim Guymer; Ralph Bailey
INTERIOR DESIGNER Guymer Bailey Architects
SUBCONTRACTORS/ SUPPLIERS Civil Engineer: Breen and Crane. Electrical and mechanical engineer: Bassetts Consulting Engineer. Structural Engineer: Glynn Tucker. Hydraulics Consultant: Richards, Ciarns and Hamilton. Buildings: Centre complex (J. Hutchinson P/L); hotel accommodation (McMaster Construction); villas, beach amenities, shopping village, staff accommodation (GW Chalmers P/L and Construction Management Associates)

NAME MAKALALI PRIVATE GAME RESERVE
ADDRESS c/o Conservation Corporation Africa, Bateleur House, 54 Wierda Road West, Wierda Valley, Sandton, Private Bag X27, Benmore, South Africa
Tel: (0)27 11 784 6832
Fax: (0)27 11 784 6207
ROOMS/FACILITIES 4 camps, 6 suites situated along the river each with Sala, and outdoor shower; public dining room, Boma, swimming pool, bar.
COMPLETION 1996
CLIENT Charles Smith
OPERATOR Conservation Corporation Africa
ARCHITECT Silvio Rech
INTERIOR DESIGNER Silvio Rech
SUBCONTRACTORS/ SUPPLIERS All work undertaken by Silvio Rech with on-site workshops and local craftsmen

NAME COMPASS POINT
ADDRESS Love Beach, Gambier, West of Cable Beach, Nassau, Bahamas
Tel: (0)809 327 4500
Fax: (0)809 327 3299
ROOMS/FACILITIES 21 roooms, 14 huts, cottages and cabanas with private deck overlooking the ocean and kitchenette; 4 studio cabanas; swimming pool; outdoor bar and restaurant; private dock with full range of water sports
COMPLETION 1995
CLIENT Island Outpost Group
OPERATOR Island Outpost Group
ARCHITECT Barbara Hulanicki
INTERIOR DESIGNER Barbara Hulanicki
SUBCONTRACTORS/ SUPPLIERS Collaborators: Island Engineering; Mary Vinson of the Island Tranding Company (bedspreads; lampshades and other furnishings)

NAME PARK HYATT TOKYO
SHINJUKA PARK TOWER
ADDRESS 3-7-1-2 Nishi Shinjuku, Shinjuku-Ku, Tokyo 163-10, Japan
Tel: (0)3 5322 1234
Fax: (0)3 5322 1288
ROOMS/FACILITIES 178 guestrooms; café; restaurant; grill; 2 bars; business centre; health centre
COMPLETION 1994
CLIENT Tokyo Gas Urban Development
OPERATOR Hyatt International Hotels
ARCHITECT Kenzo Tange Associates
INTERIOR DESIGNER John Morford & Company
SUBCONTRACTORS/ SUPPLIERS Main contractors: Kajima Corporation; Shimizu Corporation; Taisei Corporation. Architectural Lighting: Yamagiwa. Lighting Designer: John Morford & Company. Lighting suppliers: Matsushita Electric Works Ltd., Toshiba Lighting and Technology Corporation, Mitsubishi Electric Corporation. Decorative Lighting & Metal Stone Tables: Cedric Hartman. Furniture and fittings: Takashimaya (Hotel Park Hyatt)
ARTISTS Yoshitaka Echizenya, Mitsuko Mikwa, Mieko Yuli, Antony Donaldson

NAME FOUR SEASONS NEW YORK
ADDRESS 57 East 57th Street, New York, NY 1022, USA
Tel: (0)212 758 5700
Fax: (0)212 758 5711
ROOMS/FACILITIES 372 rooms, health club, restaurants, retail outlets, function rooms, business centre

COMPLETION 1993
CLIENT 57-57th Associates
OPERATOR Four Season Hotels Ltd
ARCHITECT Pei Cobb Freed & Partners; IM Pei (Partner in Charge); Eason Leonard (Partner); Leonard Jackson (Partner); Michael D. Flynn (Partner).
INTERIOR DESIGNER Chhada Siemieda & Partners; Betty Garber Design
SUBCONTRACTORS/ SUPPLIERS Associate Architect: Frank Williams Associates. Construction Manager: Tishman Construction. Consultants: Robert Rosenwasser Associates (structural); Jaros Baum & Bolles (mechanical); Fisher Marantz Renfro Stone (lighting); Cerami and Associates (acoustics); Tracy Turner Design Inc (graphics). Mechanical: Jaffie Mechanical Inc.

NAME PARK HYATT JOHANNESBURG
ADDRESS 191 Oxford Road, Rosebank 2196, South Africa
Tel: (0)11 280 1238
Fax: (0)11 280 1238
ROOMS/FACILITIES 244 rooms, 'Signature' restaurant, 'Jabulani's' wine Bar, 'No 191 at the Park' restaurant, 6 meeting rooms, 2 boardrooms, ballroom, health club
COMPLETION 1995
CLIENT Iscor Pension Fund
OPERATOR Hyatt International Corporation
ARCHITECT GAPP: Barry Senior, Chris Kroese, Johann Smith
INTERIOR DESIGNER Hirsch Bedner Associates: Howard Pharr (Director); Sandra Cortner; Randy Barras; Susasn Konkel. Project Manager: Winkfield Projects; Mike Fusedale; Willie du Plessis
SUBCONTRACTORS/ SUPPLIERS General contractor: Shoredits. Electrical Contractor: Repeat Electric. Mechanical Contractor: Northern Air. Structural Engineer: Ove Arup & Partners. Casegoods furniture: Hartman & Keppler; Modlers of Antiques; Petit Upholstery; My Design. Lighting Design: Pamboukian Associates; Paul Pamboukian. Landscape Design: OUP Associates, Johan Van Papandorf.

NAME THE FOUR SEASONS, ISTANBUL
ADDRESS Tevkifhane Sokak No. 1, 34490 Sultanahmet-Eiminonu, Istanbul, Turkey
Tel: (0)212 638 82 00.
Fax: (0)212 638 82 10
ROOMS/FACILITIES 65 rooms and suites
COMPLETION 1996
CLIENT Enternasyonel Turizm, Istanbul
OPERATOR Four Seasons Hotel Ltd
ARCHITECT Yalçin Özüekren
INTERIOR DESIGNER Metex Design Group, Sinan Kafadar (project designer)
SUBCONTRACTORS/ SUPPLIERS Main Contractor: Sultanahmet Turizm. Concrete frame: Net Yapi. Marble Work: Merpa; Atolyr G&E. Furniture in the public areas: Baker, Drexel, Beverly, Hickory Chair, Trans Century. Lighting Suppliers: Barovier Tose, Terzani, La Tulip, Erco

NAME KEMPINSKI HOTEL
TASCHENBERGPALAIS
ADDRESS Taschenberg 3, 01067 Dresden, Germany
Tel: (0)351 49 12 0
Fax: (0)351 49 12 812

ROOMS/FACILITIES 213 rooms (25 suites), Presidential suite, Business Centre, 'Intermezzo' restaurant, 'Paulaner's Bistro, Taschenberg Vestibul, 'Allegro' bar, retail outlets, banqueting facilities, conference centre, private chapel, fitness centre, heated swimming pool, pool bar, underground car park
COMPLETION 1995
CLIENT Kempinski Hotels
OPERATOR Kempinski Hotels
ARCHITECT AIC in cooperation with Planungsbüro, Versammlungsstatten
INTERIOR DESIGNER AB 'Living Design'
SUBCONTRACTORS/ SUPPLIERS General Contractor: Strabag Hoch und Ingenieurbau AG. Electrical contractor: Ingenieurgruppe Hemm. Electrical intallations: ABB Instalationen GmbH. Interior furnishing: LD Woodlink. Interior construction: Deutsche Werkstatten. Furniture: Cassina.
ARTISTS Sculptures: Lothar Beck, Christian Hempel, SHA GmbH

NAME SCHLOSSHOTEL VIER JAHRESZEITEN
ADDRESS Brahmsstrasse 10, 14193, Berlin, Germany
Tel: (0)895 84 462
Fax: (0)895 84 803
ROOMS/FACILITIES 52 room and suites, 5 banqueting halls, 'Le Jardin' restaurant, 'Vivaldi' restaurant, pool, health spa, solarium, fitness equipment, bar
COMPLETION 1995
CLIENT Residenz Grunewald GbR
OPERATOR Unternehmensgruppe Albeck & Zehden
ARCHITECT Hasso von Werder & Partner
ARTISTIC DIRECTOR Karl Lagerfeld
INTERIOR DESIGNER Ezra Attia design Ltd.
SUBCONTRACTORS/ SUPPLIERS Main contractor: BSS, Berlin. Consultants: Vernon Saunders (FF&E); Wolfgang Roth (antiques); Zilch & Partner (electricity); PKS - Werkstatten fur Denkmalpflege (restoration work). Furniture: Tempus Stet; Caledon Contract Interiors; Elder & Blythe; McLoud & Co.; Dickens of Ipswich; Kearns Furniture; Interior Selection; Harvard; William MacLean, HNB; Bernard Thorp, Charles Hunt Furnitures. Lighting: Arnold Montrose; Restall Brown & Clennell; William Mehornay Porcelain; Tindle Decorative Lighting; Besslink & Jones; Bella Figura; RBC Trading

NAME HOTEL COSTES
ADDRESS 239 rue St. Honoré, 75001 Paris, France
Tel: (0)331 42 44 5000
Fax: (0)331 42 73 34 19
ROOMS/FACILITIES 85 rooms including 4 suites and 1 apartment; restuarant; bar; swimming pool, sauna, hammam; gymnasium
COMPLETION 1995
CLIENT Jean-Louis Costes
OPERATOR Independent
ARCHITECT Mechali Architecte
INTERIOR DESIGNER Jacques Garcia
SUBCONTRACTORS/ SUPPLIERS Stonework: Emtra. Plumbing: 3C. Woodwork: Ledran. Electricity: Migdal. Paintwork: Trouve. Lighting: Societe Contraste; Jacques Garcia. Furniture Creation: Jacques Garcia; Atelier Polybe & Malet. Wallcoverings: Pierre Frey, Hodsoll Mackenzie, Nina Campbell

PHOTOGRAPHIC CREDITS

The author and the publishers would like to thank all the designers and architects involved and the photographers whose work is reproduced. The following photographic credits are given, with page numbers in brackets

Peter Aaron/Esto - used by permission of Disney Enterprises Inc. (168-9, 171); Luis Ferreira Alves (176-9); Jaime Ardiles -Arce/Courtest of The Regent Resort, Chiangmai (180-83); Architekturphoto/F. Busam (62, 64-5, 66 top, 67); Ian Atkinson/Michael Wolchover (58-9); Rinnie Bleeker (22, 25-5 top, 24 bottom); Reiner Blunck (54-7); Luc Boegly/Archipress (68-71, 82-5, 120, 122 bottom); Mark Burgin/Belle/Arcaid (184-5, 186); Rory Carnegie (34); Earl Carter/Belle/Arcaid (18, 20 top right, 20 bottom left); Louis Casals (128-31); Stafford Cliff/David Brittain - Courtesy of CD Partnership (30-33, 46-9); Courtesy of Conservation Corporation (188-91); Fernando Cerdero/Sebastian Saldiver/Courtesy of Los Cabos (133-37); Courtesy of the Clarence Hotel (50, 52, 53); Douglas Corrance (60-61); B. Davis/Courtesy Cesar Pelli & Associates (138); © Disney Enterprises, Inc. (170) Engelhardt Sellin (116-18); Courtesy of Four Seasons International (212-15); Foton Photography (202-3); Courtesy of Fukuoka-Jisho , Co. Ltd. (93); Mr Futugawa/Courtesy of Park Hyatt Tokyo (198-201); Andrew Garn (205); Marianne Haas - used by permission of Elle Decoration (224-7); Heinrich Helfentstein (121, 122 top, 123, 124-7); Arch Photo Eduard Hueber (13, 16, 17 top left, 17 bottom, 112-15); Keith Hunter (26-9); R. Greg Hursley Inc. - used by persmission of Disney Enterprises Inc. (164-7); Timothy Hursley (19, 20); Brian Janis/Phototechnik (150-3); Courtesy of Kempinski (119); Courtesy of Kingfisher Bay Resort (187); Cookie Kinhead/Island Outpost; (192-5); Jorg Klam (42, 44 top and bottom); Idris Kolodziej (63, 66 bottom) Dieter Krull (38-40); Karl Lagerfeld (221, 222 top, 223); Ake E:Son Lindman AB (108-11, 217, 219); Barry Mason (51); Peter Mauss/Esto (99-103); Maxum, Austria - Hans Wiesenhofer (72-5); Courtesy of Le Meridien Lingotto (95, 96 bottom); Ivan Muller (216-19); Osamu Murai (197 top); Nacasa & Partners, Inc/ Shotenkenchiku-sha (91, 141, 197 bottom); Courtesy of Navicom Group (14, 15, 17 top right); Robert O'Dea/Arcaid (86-9); Tomio Ohashi (104-7); Peter Paige (207 bottom); Courtesy of the Phoenix Hotel (142-5); Courtesy of Primadonna Resorts (147-9); Paul Raftery/Arcaid (94, 97); Courtesy of Rolf and Jan Rave (41, 43, 44,); Renate Ritzenhoff/Lautwein & Reitzenhoff (23, 25 bottom); T Sato/Courtesy Cesar Pelli & Associates (139, 140); Jorg Schoener (216-18); Soene (77-81); Courtesy of Studio Sofield (98); Ydo Sol (220, 222 below); Courtesy of Sun International (158-63); Courtesy of Sunway Lagoon Resort (154-7); Toyota Photo Studio (90, 92); Vittoria Kartisek of Vittoria Visuals (172); Morley von Sternberg (35); Michael Wilson Architectural Photography; Kim Zwartz (37)

INDEX OF PROJECTS, ARCHITECTS AND DESIGNERS